The Vengeance of Medea. [A novel.]

Edith Wheelwright

The Vengeance of Medea. [A novel.]
Wheelwright, Edith
British Library, Historical Print Editions
British Library
1894].
290 p. ; 8°.
012629.ee.7.

The BiblioLife Network

This project was made possible in part by the BiblioLife Network (BLN), a project aimed at addressing some of the huge challenges facing book preservationists around the world. The BLN includes libraries, library networks, archives, subject matter experts, online communities and library service providers. We believe every book ever published should be available as a high-quality print reproduction; printed on- demand anywhere in the world. This insures the ongoing accessibility of the content and helps generate sustainable revenue for the libraries and organizations that work to preserve these important materials.

The following book is in the "public domain" and represents an authentic reproduction of the text as printed by the original publisher. While we have attempted to accurately maintain the integrity of the original work, there are sometimes problems with the original book or micro-film from which the books were digitized. This can result in minor errors in reproduction. Possible imperfections include missing and blurred pages, poor pictures, markings and other reproduction issues beyond our control. Because this work is culturally important, we have made it available as part of our commitment to protecting, preserving, and promoting the world's literature.

GUIDE TO FOLD-OUTS, MAPS and OVERSIZED IMAGES

In an online database, page images do not need to conform to the size restrictions found in a printed book. When converting these images back into a printed bound book, the page sizes are standardized in ways that maintain the detail of the original. For large images, such as fold-out maps, the original page image is split into two or more pages.

Guidelines used to determine the split of oversize pages:

• Some images are split vertically; large images require vertical and horizontal splits.
• For horizontal splits, the content is split left to right.
• For vertical splits, the content is split from top to bottom.
• For both vertical and horizontal splits, the image is processed from top left to bottom right.

THE VENGEANCE OF MEDEA

The Vengeance of Medea

BY

EDITH GRAY WHEELWRIGHT

LONDON

DIGBY, LONG & CO., PUBLISHERS

18 BOUVERIE STREET, FLEET STREET, E.C.

TO

A. C. E.

Dear little friend, whose truth and loyalty
Have never changed with time, take this, and pray
That I, the richer for your love, may grow
More worthy; that from out the humble round
Of work and pure endeavour, some fair growth
Of Wisdom may arise to bless with joy
And fruitfulness, the changeful course of years.

CONTENTS.

——o——

The Vengeance of Medea

——◆——

CHAPTER I.

'Behold, I dream a dream of good,
And mingle all the world with thee.'—TENNYSON.

'This is the great task of Life also, to discern things
and divide them, and say, " Outward things are not in my
power, but to will is in my power." '
Teaching of EPICTETUS.

THE wind had ceased, and the eye of the earth closed gently upon crowded lands and peaceful valleys where Nature lay at rest.

It was twilight in the northern hemisphere— tall oaks and cedars wavered in uncertain outlines against a paling sky; sleep movements began to stir among the flowers beds, delicate leaves were folded against the chills of the summer night, where here and there an evening primrose stood erect and stately in mute invitation to her nocturnal guest.

A

From an upper window in a pretty English home, an elderly man sat looking out into the shadows. He was propped up with cushions, for he was very weak, and the hand which had waved encouragement from a commander's saddle at Peshawur lay shrivelled and inert by his side. Yet the eyes had not lost their brilliancy, and the expression of the bronzed face bore unshrinking witness to a life of honourable days. There was a smile upon his lips at this moment, as some old memory flashed up from the shadows now closing round his life, and his thoughts had wandered back to these open-handed days of Indian experience—of lavish hospitality, of political unrest, of desperate struggle and hand-to-hand fight with treacherous and unknown foes. Memories, too, of other days were with him—days serene and peaceful under Italian skies, hallowed by the love of a sweet and constant nature, and saddened at last by an irrevocable loss.

The old soldier's hand closed suddenly upon a letter he was holding, and it recalled him sharply to the present time and the few duties yet remaining for his faltering energies to fulfil. In the sum of his well-spent and successful life there lingered still some leaven of anxiety. He was a father and a guardian: the responsible attitude, with all its by-gone sweetness, weighed upon his soul. He turned away from the window with a short sigh, and at that moment a slender maiden entered, bearing a small, shaded lamp in her hand.

'Dear old dad, sitting so patiently in the darkness,' she said cheerily. 'I have come to interrupt your intercourse with the owls.'

'That is right. I wanted my little girl and was about to ring for her,' said the Colonel, and he watched the graceful little figure in its gyrations as Sybil began, in a peculiarly rapid fashion, to close the blinds and rearrange the details of the room.

'Don't turn *all* the chairs upside down, please, little woman,' observed the invalid mildly after a moment's pause, 'and I don't think the carpet need be swept until to-morrow.'

Sybil halted in a somewhat aimless adjustment of an antimacassar, and shook her auburn curls. Then she came and knelt by the Colonel's side in such a manner that the light, falling athwart her shoulders, left her face in shade. For the fact was that her hazel eyes were dimmed with recent weeping, and the brave little loving heart was trying to mask its sorrow by an assumed gaiety of tone. Oh pathos of such endeavour! In its anxious attempt at subterfuge it deceives itself alone.

'There has been a letter, Sybil,' said the old man very gently, 'from Miss Wellton. I want to talk

to you about it once more—for the last time. No,
don't interrupt me, dear ; let me fulfil my duties
while I can. The matter is all but decided, and
the casting vote remains with you—you and Michal.'

'Shall I call the Poetess ?' said Sybil quickly,
and she rose and hurried to the door.

Her summons was soon answered. The elder girl
took her place also by her guardian's couch, and
the light from the little lamp shone softly in the
black depths of her eyes and on her coronet of silky
hair.

The old soldier looked up at her with a strange
expression as his hand rested tremblingly on her
dark head.

Michal Iliff was his ward ; on her mother's side
she was of Italian parentage, of her father,
nothing was ever heard. Thus her history, as the
world knew it, was a simple one, but that other
story, fraught with so many issues that had been
woven about her life in its infancy, was known to
very few. And although the Colonel had ever
been unvaryingly tender and indulgent towards his
motherless daughter, Sybil, yet there was something in his manner towards her dark-eyed com-
rade which betrayed a deeper feeling still.

'I wanted to talk to you about this letter,' he
began again. 'It is from Miss Wellton. She says
that she can easily arrange to give you your

rooms such as you would require, and the terms and all other details seem satisfactory. Of course, I felt sure that they would do so. I know the house, which is a pleasant one, and Miss Sally herself is the embodiment of highly correct citizenship, but I wanted to ask you both once more before deciding finally. Is my little girl fixed in her resolution?'

Sybil looked up, and met the passionate gaze of the dark eyes opposite. Moved by the same sudden impulse, the two girls clasped hands.

'Quite fixed,' said Sybil gently.

'It is true,' resumed the Colonel after a pause, 'that if the life does not suit you, you are not bound irrevocably to it. Neither will you be subjected to the strain and struggle for a livelihood which is the lot of most artists who seek for success and fame. My little girl will always have her income to fall back upon, and it is sufficient. It is also secured, so that my mind is easy on that score, while Michal, of course—' his glance rested for an instant upon the pale aristocratic face, and there was a tremor in his voice as he concluded—'Michal, of course, has hers.'

Thereafter, silence.

Sybil was struggling bravely to say something in an even tone, but the flesh and the will were at war.

'The Poetess,' she began falteringly, 'is a tower of strength. You need never be afraid for me, Daddy darling, as long as she and I are together; and our lives have "together twined," you know. She will never be engulfed in the whirlpool of artistic ruin, will you, my Poetess?'

'No whirlpools shall engulf either of us, *cara mia*, if I can prevent it,' said the musical voice of Michal.

'Sublime optimism of youth,' answered the Colonel smiling, 'and of poets. Well, then, it appears that I am to give you the first lift upon the ladder of a professional career. I do not oppose it, mind, even in thought. I have too sound a faith in the wisdom and capability of each of you, and a life of active work, with a steady aim, is perhaps the best training for women as well as for men. I do not oppose it. I only wish that there had been some one able to guide you sometimes with a bit of cheery advice—some artist, perhaps, who could have helped you. My cousin, Jane Charlecote, will be ready enough to pilot you through the maze of social life, but she is no more good in the artistic line than a battery of artillery.'

Sybil hesitated a moment.

'Mr Vernon,' she said, 'told me, you know, daddy, to write to him if ever I wanted help—I mean, if ever I went to London. I don't think I should like to do that, but perhaps we may meet him again some day—'

The honest face of the old soldier was a little clouded.

'I don't know Leslie Vernon,' he answered slowly, 'and what I have heard about him, I don't quite understand. There is something rather odd, somehow, in the idea of an Academician of his standing offering to give you lessons in that off-hand sort of way. One would have supposed, too, that after his kindness to you on your sketching tour that week, he would have accepted my invitation, instead of rejecting it—not churlishly, perhaps, but still with a lack of geniality. Well, never mind now; we all have our peculiarities. I am a bluff old fellow myself—somewhat too free, I dare-say—and do not understand these reserved sort of men.'

'Mr Vernon is a strange person,' said Michal quietly, 'but I think he means what he says.'

She had noticed a flush of pained perplexity on the fair cheek of her friend, and had hastened to supply her answer. The Colonel sank back upon his pillows with a gesture of weariness. Sybil sprang to her feet.

'You have talked long enough, daddy dear,' she said gently, 'and are growing tired. Shall I fetch a book to read to you a little while?'

'No; there is something I have still to say to Michal,' he answered faintly.

The old restlessness was stealing back into his eyes.

'You shall say it to-morrow,' said his adopted daughter with tender emphasis, and, yielding to her will, he rested.

CHAPTER II.

'Turn to the annals of a former day.'—BYRON.

'LORD REA said:—" Well! God mend all!"' '" Nay,"
said Sir David Ramsay, " we must help Him to mend it."'

'THE Colonel has something on his mind, Miss
Iliff, which he wishes to say to you,' said the nurse
as she met Michal, on the following day, coming
from her guardian's room.

'I know; he has just told me so. The doctor
thought that he had better indulge his wish this
afternoon, so I intend to return to him immediately. Will you not take a walk in the interval?'

And Michal went quietly back to the Colonel's
room. He greeted her expectantly. His voice
was stronger than it had been on the previous
night, and his whole bearing gave evidence of
a suppressed excitement. Michal noted it and
thought with a pang of the doctor's verdict—'It
may be a question of days or of weeks. Don't be

9

deceived by fitful flashes of vigour.'   She stood by
the bed, looking down lovingly from her great dark
eyes, while Sybil, her head resting on her hand, sat
near.

The Colonel took the long, white fingers of the
Poetess in his own shrunken palm very tenderly.

'I want to tell you, my dear,' he said, 'the story
of your birth and childhood.   You have not yet
heard it, and my days are numbered now.'

The girl drew a quick breath as she listened—
the proud lips closed in a firm and rigid line.

Sybil rose as though to leave them, but a glance
from the Poetess made her pause.

'Not so, darling,' said Michal gently.   'You
have shared my ignorance all these years; will
you not share my knowledge now—whether for
good or evil?'

Sybil silently sat down.

'Yes,' said the Colonel thoughtfully, 'that is
better so.   I have only kept you in ignorance of
your parentage all these years, my dear, because
there seemed no reason to disturb our happy relationship with thoughts other than of peace, and I
knew well enough what impression the story
would leave upon you.   Now, the case is different;
I have come to the end of my tether, and you
should know it.   Sybil is like your own sister, too.'

'We are more than sisters,' said Michal, and the

mellow cadence of her beautiful voice set the common-place words to music.

'Well, then, before Sybil was born,' said the Colonel, breaking in hurriedly, as though fearful of losing precious time, 'we were in Florence—my wife and I—spending the winter there. I was home on furlough, and we had not been married long. There were no claims to call us elsewhere in those halcyon days, and we spent a perfectly happy time together'—a shadow crossed the old soldier's face as he spoke—'a perfectly happy time. It was in March, I think, when the incident happened which was to influence your after life. You are standing, my dear—why not sit down?'

But Michal, whose tall figure stood erect and motionless as a statue, made a hasty movement of dissent, and the Colonel proceeded with his tale.

'We were walking—my Jeannie and I—from Fiesole one afternoon when we saw, by the roadside, a woman of the peasant class lying apparently insensible. She had a young child in her arms—a little, dark-haired girl—and as my wife stopped for a moment to see whether it might be a case demanding the sympathy of a stranger, the little one stretched out its arms with a cry. That was quite enough for the tender heart of my

Jeannie. She took up the poor wee thing and soothed it, and we began to make inquiries about the woman, and had her conveyed to her home.'

A pause. The Colonel's voice grew stronger, and his language more eloquent. He seemed to have forgotten the present in the vivid interest of those by-gone days. He was living again in the fair Italian city, the companion of his love was again beside him, a little, dark-haired child in her arms.

'She was very ill, poor woman,' he continued slowly; 'dying, the doctor said. We visited her many times during her illness, and then we heard her story. It appeared that, four years previously, a young English nobleman had stayed for some time in Florence, accompanied by a friend. He was a gay young fellow, fresh from college, with plenty of money to fling about and plenty of time to misuse, and he saw Lucia Safrana in an evil hour, and fell in love with her. She was a remarkably hand-some girl, that poor Lucia—such a figure! with the dark eyes, too, and rich colouring of the South. She was a peasant lass, a Contadina, and was naturally flattered by the attentions of the young English lord. I believe she loved him—passion-ately, jealously, as Italians love. Anyhow, they were married.'

Another pause. The girl standing by the bedside was mute and motionless—Sybil watched her with wide and anxious eyes.

'They were married,' said the Colonel again. 'I don't know how it was all managed, or what was represented to the young Earl's friends. He was of age, of course, and in possession of his father's title. He and Lucia left Florence soon afterwards, and travelled from place to place in Italy. Then suddenly, after a year or so, the young husband was mysteriously summoned home, while Lucia returned to Florence with her child, well and happy. She expected her husband to return in about three months' time. He had represented to her that the journey was a disagreeable one,—a duty, not a pleasure—that he should be free to return to her when his business matters were settled. The idea of taking his peasant wife home with him never seems to have entered his head. Then, of course, there followed the inevitable awakening. He had left her, not for a time, but for life. A companionship so ill assorted had proved unendurable and had worn out its charms and romance.

A letter came from him explaining all the difficulties and trials of his position, the sacrifices that were extorted by custom and society from a man of his high rank; the lands, the houses, the seat in Parliament, the whole curriculum of public life must and would fall upon his shoulders. Lucia would understand that to share such burdens would render life unendurable; it would ruin both herself and him. How much better for him to return to her, as he should assuredly do, in the interval of peace which his busy life might some day afford him! There, I don't remember it all, but Lucia, poor thing, gave us the letter to read—it was written in passable Italian. There had been bank notes, too, inside it—notes which she had torn with her teeth and trampled on. In the first frenzy of her rage and disappointment they told me she would have killed her child also. Then her mood changed, and from that time one sole idea possessed her. She would go to England and be revenged, no matter how great the difficulties, how long the time to be spent in preparation. She began to work feverishly, saving up every spare earning, and then this illness came on. She was utterly exhausted and broken. She seemed to have no love, no tenderness left in her, not even for her little, dark-haired *Michal*.'

The tall, motionless figure was swayed by some sudden movement. Sybil rose, with an action of gentlest sympathy, and stood by her friend's side.

'Did she die?' asked the elder girl in a low voice.

'What, Lucia? Yes, I imagine so. It happened like this. My wife and I were summoned to

England—Jeannie's father was seriously ill, we could not delay our journey—but before we left we offered to adopt the little Michal and to bring her up as our own child. She was a winsome little creature, and my Jeannie had taken to her in a wonderful way. Quixotic, of course, people called us, and other names less agreeable, but we never cared a straw about that. We only knew that the mother lay dying, and the child would grow up neglected and uncared for, and we took the wee thing with us. The Padre who visited Lucia promised to write and let us know if Lucia recovered, but no letter has ever come—indeed, we never expected it—and no tidings from that day to this of Lucia.'

'And my father?' asked Michal quietly.

She spoke without any apparent emotion, but Sybil knew that a tumult of passions lay buried beneath the calm. The Colonel's face darkened.

'I have not spoken of that man for years,' he said abruptly. 'I can hardly speak of him now without letting out fire, but it ill becomes a man on his death-bed to speak hard words of his neighbour, so I will say as little as I can. I went to him, and during that interview I said things that were perhaps unnecessary, for the cold politeness of the man put my back up, and I was always a blundering sort of fellow, too ready to speak out my mind. So we had an unpleasant encounter, and before the end of it I got at his weak point. He had married a woman of high family within the year after his return, and had given out that his wife was dead. There was no evidence to prove the contrary—the peasant woman living so far away, in a foreign country, had no power to contradict his tale. He was just starting out on an ambitious political career, and the story which I told him of Lucia's illness and probable death, and of my adoption of the little Michal, fell upon unwilling ears. He had washed his hands of his first ill-assorted marriage, he had no desire to confess publicly the existence of his child. He is spoken of now as the proudest and most immaculate nobleman in the Upper House—he may be — and a man of most stainless honour, but never mind that now. He promised to pay three hundred pounds per annum to my bankers as long as his daughter lived. He was ready to do anything, pay anything, to ensure my secrecy. I accepted the terms and left him. You know the rest, my dears. We left for India soon afterwards, and little Michal, of course, went too. Then our Sybil was born to us, and altogether I consider that I have had the best of the bargain.' He held out his hand, as he spoke, to Michal. 'Mine has been the joy that your father renounced,' he said tenderly, and I have never regretted it, my dear, for a day. Sybil's life, too, has been enriched by the love of a sister, and my loss has been softened by the devotion of my girls.'

Sybil's auburn curls touched his hand caressingly, her bright eyes shone with tears. Not that the story seemed, to her light-hearted philosophy, so very dreadful after all. If Michal's father *were* a bad man, she reflected gravely, what did it matter to them as long as they had nothing to do with him? The Poetess, as she loved to call her friend, had become a part of her own life. What could anything matter?

But the pride of the father awoke again in the sensitive soul of Michal; to her the revelation was fraught with intense and bitter pain.

There was silence for a space, while the Colonel rested on his pillows a little wearily.

'I think I have told you everything,' he said at length. 'Your income, you see, is assured, and though you may never meet your father, yet it was right that you should know from what source that income was derived. His name though, I have not yet told you—the Earl—'

'Stay,' cried the Poetess. 'I will not know his name. If once I knew it, and should ever, in some evil hour, cross his path, it would be bad equally for me and for him. I, the daughter of his peasant wife, would speak as *she* would probably have spoken. I, too, have southern blood and can love and hate intensely, but I do not wish to forget, as he has done, that "*noblesse oblige*," and I will not hear his name.'

The Colonel pondered. He had always been accustomed to yield to the passionate impulses and strong will of his adopted daughter; he was also accustomed to trust her judgments when formed. At this moment, therefore, it was not likely that he could oppose her wish, and he yielded.

'Be it as you will, my dear,' he answered gently. If at any time you should alter your determination, the means of attaining the knowledge lie, of course, in your own hands. In my small iron box are papers which will prove the main facts in my narrative, and among them is also a necklace given by your father to Lucia. She insisted, poor soul, upon our taking that relic; a ring which he had given her she kept, and his letters also, but the necklace we brought away. There would be no harm in your looking at it, my dear. There is the box yonder, on my table; the key is with others in my drawer. You can fetch it, Sybil.'

'Do look, Poetess,' said the younger girl softly, and Michal reluctantly obeyed.

The box was brought and opened, and the necklace—a slight, but beautiful, thing of delicate gold workmanship—was disclosed.

Sybil looked with naïve curiosity at it and at the old documents lying beneath. Michal glanced at both in silence, and the box was soon replaced. Then the Poetess went again to the bedside, a wonderful softness dwelling in her deep, dark eyes.

'*Padre mio*,' she said gently, and her flexible voice lingered in mellow cadence upon the sweet Italian words, 'the little child you rescued thanks you for the tender care of all these years. She has ever loved you as a father, now her gratitude is at least as great as her love.'

'Never mind about that; the love makes us quits, my dear,' said the Colonel.

CHAPTER III.

'I go to prove my soul.   I see my way,
   As birds their trackless way.   I shall arrive.'
                                    BROWNING.

EVENING mists lay lightly over the weary earth;
the harvest fields were sleeping beneath the veil,
the wayward breezes wandered in sweet restlessness upon the meadows where the children played,
and o'er the woods where the forest poets lay
silently within their sheltered nests.   It was the
'Arn Monat' of our ancestors, and the rich gifts
of golden-haired Demeter stood ripening for the
eager sickle of the labouring man.

In the vineyards of the South, the trellised
vines grew purple.   Those are stately memories—
memories linking us with the remotest past—that
dwell among the harvest fields; the thoughts of
the sower are long, long thoughts, but the reaper
looks ever backward.

Down by the little stream, where the bulrush
and the reed mace grew, and the purple loosestrife

20

raised its clustered spikes above the reed-fringed margin, a solitary bird poured forth its low, quick song.

No other sound broke the stillness. The far blue fields slept in the loosed raiment of Nature's restful hour; tiny leaves, luminous with dew, clung motionless to the sod ; among the barren moss late violets were hidden.

The oaks were silent, and only the breath of the evening was tuneful with that one articulate song.

But presently, white rifts of light appeared as rents and patches among the dusky clouds, heralding, with their shreds of scattered silver, the crowning glory of a mighty moon. Then the pale forget-me-nots stirred as the bright beams kissed them, and the long-leaved rushes whispered in elfish cadences, while their edges shone like silver threads.

Two girls lingered by the grassy margin, listening to the warbler's song. The meadow circled round their pretty garden ; here, in earth's sweet solitudes, they loved to linger, and hither they had wandered now. They stood together talking as those alone can talk whose hearts are united in that pure bond of friendship which is Heaven's choicest gift to poor humanity. Nothing had come between them all their lives to mar their perfect union, and yet they differed in character just as the birds differ in plumage, and habit and song. And now they were standing on that fateful ground which, in most human lives, has proved to be the crisis, and is marked by the sign-post of uncertainty, at the crossing of the roads.

One of them stood erect, dauntless, with burning gaze ready to pierce, it might be, all worlds and their mysteries, all knowledge and all pain. The other, cast in lighter mould, glanced fearfully into the veiled unknown, and trembled.

'Success is so rare, Poetess,' she said wistfully. 'How dare we hope for it?'

'We do not hope,' said the elder girl, her rich tones full of passion. 'We do not snatch it as did Prometheus his fire. Success is in ourselves. We must aim high, impatient at our nothingness, content only with the purest ideals, the noblest life.'

'I am not like you, my Poetess,' said little Sybil, looking up in simple admiration at the earnest, dreaming eyes. 'My mind casts a lesser shade. You will conquer in the struggle, for you are strong and worthy. I have no genius, I can only work— and love.'

Michal stooped and gathered,' a spray of pale forget-me-nots.

'Thy life shall chant its own beatitudes,' she said gently, and Sybil took the flowers in silence from her hand.

The sweet, southern breeze sighed lightly through the foliage; the sedge warbler still crooned its melody into the quiet night, but the air was growing chill.

Slowly, therefore, and with some reluctance, the two girls retraced their steps, bearing with them a memory that stirred thereafter at the sight of blue forget-me-nots, and whose chords vibrated at a fragment of the little warbler's song.

CHAPTER IV

'Should auld acquaintance be forgot?'

GREAT upheavals had been witnessed in the house in Maida Vale.

Miss Wellton, known to her intimates as 'Miss Sally,' was a somewhat nervous, elderly person of respectability unimpeachable, of decayed fortune, and of severest ethical code. Her boarding establishment was a praiseworthy example of the survival of the fittest among the many competitors, inasmuch as it had kept its owner's head above water for thirty years, and had been the favourite resort of a variegated respectability, from the well-to-do widow or spinster, to that less popular class of gentlewoman known in society as 'decayed.'

But the increasing competition had affected even the sure foundations of the house in Maida Vale, and Miss Sally was not sorry to complete an arrangement which would ensure to her such desir-

able boarders as Colonel Murray's daughter and
ward.

It was therefore with an unusual degree of care-
fulness that she made the necessary preparation for
their comfort. The two bedrooms were perfect in
detail, the carpets, with faded cabbage roses and
carnations, memorials of better days, when Miss
Sally's little world was young ; days, too, before
'high art' and its accessories of Kensington Art-
ware and curtain frills, of milk stools and high
mantelpieces, had invaded the more solid fashions
of mahogany and chintz.

Miss Sally, during the last thirty years, had kept
house, not for herself, but for the multitude ; she
had learnt many things during her probation; she
had adapted herself to innovations of many kinds,
but there was a limit to such adaptation, and her
steadfast soul refused to bow at the shrine of high
art.

She watched the arrival of her new guests' be-
longings with the mild curiosity that even her
chequered experience had not been entirely able
to suppress.

One dusky October day had seen the arrival of
a piano, which was placed in the smaller of the two
sitting-rooms which communicated by folding-doors.
Miss Sally knew that it was the desire of her new
boarders to live apart from the rest of the establish-

ment; she knew also that Miss Murray was an artist, and she had arranged accordingly to give them these two rooms on the ground floor.

During the ensuing fortnight her attention was much distracted by the various articles of furniture that were deposited by the railway van at her door.

There was a mighty easel, an equally extensive bookcase, a deck chair, an easy chair, an oak escritoire, cases of ornaments, multitudinous rugs, and cases of books that were positively alarming.

The good woman hovered about them with occasional exclamations of subdued wonder, and they afforded some material for conversation in which the two other boarders also shared.

But after the arrival of the two girls, a wondrous transformation was developed in the neat and solemn rooms, and they seemed to burst forth into a new exuberance of youth and bright activity.

Pictures, china, and Indian ornaments adorned the sober walls; beautiful Indian knick-knacks and oriental curiosities filled odd corners; richly-coloured rugs and tiger-skins made the carnations in the carpet run to seed; glowing patches of colour here and there shone through the dim atmosphere.

Books and paints and music, and the flowers which were never absent from the table, testified to the cheery presence of two refined and intelligent inmates.

It was the end of April; the wheels of the great metropolis had been once more greased to enter upon the ceaseless race of fashionable and political life. The tender emerald of new-born foliage was spreading over the parks and plantations; the baskets of the flower-girls were radiant with the promise of the spring, and the town houses of the *beau monde* had once more emerged from their hibernation of dulness and repose.

'Now, my Poetess, abandon that ponderous literature, and come back, if you can, "to this base earth from the firmament," and give me a cup of tea.'

So spoke the cheery voice of Sybil Murray, as she entered the room suddenly one afternoon.

'Tea?' said Michal, absently looking up at the little graceful figure divesting itself of its superfluous wraps.

'Yes, tea. Why, Poetess, you are half asleep,' was the quick rejoinder. 'I don't believe you know there is toast on the table, and I saw those water-cresses the moment I came in. Do wake up, there's a dear, Poetess, I have such a lot to tell you about the studio to-day.'

Michal rose with a bright smile.

'I had forgotten that you would return so soon,

cara mia. Sit down at once and tell me everything —my absorption in Mill's essay made me oblivious of the water-cresses. Now we will have the re-action. Tell me about your day.'

And as she presided at the tea-table, and listened with sympathetic comments to the stream of anecdote that fell from Sybil's lips, Michal thought that she had never seen the fair face opposite to her look more fair. Sybil was re-covering from the pain and sense of loss that the summer days of the previous year had brought to her. Her black dress, falling in graceful folds about her slender figure, set off the brightness of her auburn hair, the golden brown eyes sparkled under their long lashes. There was a perpetual radiation of gladness from Sybil; joy was as natural to her as song is to the blackbird—it was the reflection of a pure and happy soul.

'Poetess, I have had the first *real* word of praise to-day,' she said impressively. 'Mr Raffini stopped as he was passing my easel, and said, "That is well drawn." Do you know, that bit of spontaneity put fresh life into me, Poetess. It leavened the whole day.'

Michal nodded.

'Oh! and I heard some of the girls talking,' continued Sybil. 'They were talking about Leslie Vernon.'

'Ah!' Michal's eyes were attentive.

'They were saying all sorts of horrid things about him, Poetess. They call him "the Bear with the Ragged Staff," in joke (you remember the great notched stick he carries with him?); and they say there is no end to his eccentricity. He only paints by fits and starts. This year he exhibits only two pictures—both very small. His models seem to be the only people who speak well of him.'

'And what did you say?' asked the Poetess.

'I said nothing. I did not know what to say. These two girls were talking with Mr Raffini, you know. I have never spoken much to either of them, and did not like to break into the conversation and contradict them. We have only known Mr Vernon for a week upon a sketching tour, and they have known him, probably, for years. Besides—'

'Besides, you did not wish to furnish food for caricature in your sketches of our tour and its adventures,' said Michal, smiling. 'You were doubtless right, and yet—*I* should have fallen straight into Scylla or Charybdis, and have told them all about your sprained ankle and Mr Vernon's timely help.'

'Yes, you are braver than I am,' said Sybil, gravely, but she soon brightened again.

'Shall we have a day at the National Gallery on Saturday, Poetess?' she said.

Michal assented readily. She, too, loved to wander among the silent monuments of genius which Art has given to the world, and her love of the beautiful was intense.

'I am glad you did not take Leslie Vernon at his word,' she said presently. 'I am glad you found a footing for yourself without asking his advice. And he is just the man to applaud such independence, if he knew of it.'

'I think you are right,' said Sybil.

There were not many people lingering about the silent gallery on that Saturday afternoon. The great rooms were almost deserted, and the pale saints—those deathless embodiments of mediæval zeal—seemed to chill, with the cold breath of their other-worldliness, the throbbing heart of modern man.

But in the water-colour rooms there were a few visitors wandering idly round the Turner Collection and one of these stood apart from the rest in a corner, gazing with intense scrutiny at a sketch upon the wall.

This was a tall man, spare in figure, and of a striking countenance, betokening a somewhat complex disposition.

His thick brown hair fell away from a deeply-furrowed brow, below which two dark eyes wandered restlessly. The lips were finely curved, and set in an expression of stern and implacable reserve. He wore a velvet jacket no longer in its prime, and his whole costume showed an uncompromising defiance of custom and Bond Street tailors.

And now he stood with his hands thrust deep into his pockets, frowning at the sketch before him.

'Wonderful!' he muttered, half aloud; 'the perfect "abandon" of spontaneity, combined with supremest skill! It is but a finger-mark of genius, but it has the sacred fire.'

Pondering on this theme, he moved away slowly, with eyes bent on the ground, and, as he moved, his glance idly followed the track of a shadow cast by two figures who were standing against the opposite wall.

The sunlight was not excessive, and the shadow was feeble at its best, still he followed it half-unconsciously, till it was lost in the black folds of a gown.

Then he paused abruptly, and the joy of sudden recognition in his deep eyes changed to a look of pain.

He stood for a minute hesitating, and then cast the die. He walked forward and held out his hand.

'What, Mr Vernon?' cried Sybil, as she and the Poetess turned round suddenly at the sound of a voice that they knew. 'How funny!'

'Very. I am glad to see that you still take a cheerful view of life,' said Leslie Vernon.

Michal greeted him composedly. Sybil, who was more easily surprised, grew nervous, and at a loss for words.

'We have met in an appropriate spot,' said Michal, pleasantly.

'That is meant, I imagine, as a compliment to myself,' returned the artist, drily, 'though, as far as you are concerned, the British Museum reading-room—not to suggest Mount Olympus—might have been more appropriate still. On what errand, may I ask, are you hither bound? On another sketching tour?'

'No; we have come to London,' said Michal, simply, 'to live.'

The artist glanced quickly at both girls, and noted their mourning for the first time.

'I beg your pardon,' he said, in a softened voice. 'I had not observed—I am very sorry.'

'Thank you,' said Sybil.

He looked for an instant into the clear, sweet eyes, and his own fell.

'Have you been here long?' was his next question.

'Since October.'

'And you are—at work?'

'Yes, in Raffini's studio.'

Sybil raised her eyes with a bright gleam of triumph, and, having once started upon the subject, she went on merrily to give a comprehensive sketch of their London life and its developments.

The artist listened in silence. It was impossible to judge from his stern, set face whether the narrative gave him pleasure or pain—whether he was indifferent or interested.

But at the end he said: 'Brave little girl,' and Michal saw that the lines about his mouth had relaxed somewhat. For the Poetess could be an observant person when she chose.

'And you,' he said, abruptly turning to Michal, 'daughter of the Muses, how fares it with you during the long hours of your friend's probation? You sit surrounded, I suppose, by Ruskin, Milton and Dante, and a heterogenous collection of satellites, and you forget your meals and the time of day?'

'I shall not contradict you,' said the Poetess smiling. '"Thy wit is a most sharp sauce."'

'Then it is the only redeeming quality in a mental waste,' said the artist carelessly, 'and I trust to your charity to overlook its density. So you are living in Maida Vale?' (He took down the

C

address hurriedly). 'You are near neighbours of mine; I live in St John's Wood, and, if ever I feel an ardent desire to renew my long-lost association with Dante, may I take advantage of Miss Iliff's presence?'

'You may,' said the Poetess.

Slowly the two girls moved away, both a trifle graver than was their wont. The accidental meeting had brought back some vivid memories of their happy summer tour. The acquaintance with Leslie Vernon, begun so easily with an act of simple kindness on his part, had ripened sooner than such acquaintances often do. There had then ensued a pause when they had heard nothing of him, and now—

'He is as odd as ever, Poetess,' said Sybil, a little rippling smile breaking through her seriousness. 'Fancy dressing like that in London.'

'That,' said Michal, 'is a triviality. There should be perfect freedom in the matter of dress.'

Sybil shook her head doubtfully; she was not inclined for argument, but this was one of the many points where she and her friend diverged.

Mrs Grundy was more than a spectre to little Sybil, and whereas the Poetess, in her independent life, lived to a great extent uninfluenced by custom, the gentler spirit of the younger girl succumbed to the strong bias of environment.

Thus they differed ever, but the difference never tended to mar the full harmony of their lives.

And the man in the velvet jacket walked hurriedly along the crowded thoroughfares to his solitary home.

He walked with his head bowed, his stern glance bent earthwards, as was his custom when strongly moved.

'Fool! fool!' he was saying to himself bitterly, between his set teeth. 'Led on once more by a shadow! as though life and its bitterness had not cured me of such folly. I had crushed it down all these months and thought I had killed it—why has it come to mock me now?'

Out of the crowd and bustle there rose a memory before his lurid eyes :—

'What, Mr Vernon?' said a fresh young voice, 'how funny!'

He tried to laugh it down, but could not.

'I will have one more look at those golden eyes,' he said to himself—'and then—'

CHAPTER V.

'There are two elements that go to the composition of friendship, each so sovereign that I can detect no superiority in either—one is Truth, the other, Tenderness.'

EMERSON.

'LADY CHARLECOTE, please, miss,' said the trim housemaid who ushered the pleasant-faced, old lady, one Saturday afternoon, into the presence of Sybil and her friend.

'Well, my dears,' said the visitor genially, as she advanced to greet the girls. 'My first call has been long delayed, but I could not help that. I have only lately returned from the Riviera; and then there was the house-painting bother, and Sir John has been laid up with a cold. Altogether, I have had my hands full. And now I suppose you are settled—not bad rooms (though it *is* the other end of nowhere)—and what I want to know is, *what* are you doing with yourselves?'

The old lady's volubility was a cloak for a series of remarkably shrewd observations. She had made

36

up her mind, during this first speech, that, although
Sybil was a very pretty young woman, and would
do her credit as a distant relative, Michal Iliff (of
whose parentage she was not aware) would do her
greater credit still, by virtue of her intense originality.

All the time that she kept up a brisk flow of conversation with Sybil, her sharp eyes were taking
the measure of the Poetess, who remained passive
under the scrutiny. Michal's black dress was relieved by a folded muslin scarf about her shoulders ;
the rich outlines of her figure were not disguised
by the simplicity of her gown ; the proud, aristocratic head wore its natural coronet of silky hair ;
the face, though not beautiful, was uncommon, and
Lady Charlecote recognised its charm.

'You have a lot of the old things about you, I
see,' pursued the visitor, glancing at the tiger-skin
that enveloped Michal's chair. 'Poor, dear Frank,
how fond he was of collecting things. And your
piano, I see, is in the next room, and a great easel.
Ah, yes! I had forgotten this artistic scheme. Do
you really go to a regular school, my dear, and
learn? I should have thought it would have been
very tedious.'

'I love it,' said Sybil, with the sudden fire of a
creature who stands at bay. 'It is my life.'

'Ah! yes; girls must have some hobby now-a-

days—till they marry. And you, also, my dear?
Have you—what do you call it?—a "life"?'

'My energies are not localised,' said Michal,
shrinking a little as from an alien pressure upon a
sensitive place; 'but I am rarely idle.'

'Bless me,' said the old lady testily; 'of course
you are not. Nobody ever is in this *fin-de-siècle*
rush and uproar. What everybody is the better for
so much work, *I* cannot see.'

'Is not that a rather common platitude of the
age?' said Michal. 'Did you ever know anyone,
dear Lady Charlecote, better for a life of idleness?'

The charm of the Poetess softened the opposition of her words, but the little visitor did not relish
the sound of them. They savoured of "advanced"
views, to her thinking, and she looked again at
Michal.

'You must come to my "at homes,"' she said
decidedly. 'Young girls should not work themselves to death, and pick up queer notions. You
will meet some charming young men at my house,
I can assure you.'

'You are very good. That, indeed, will be a
new experience in the *fin-de-siècle*,' said Sybil, with
laughing sarcasm.

The old lady laughed.

'Ah! my dear, we must take the world as we
find it; its streets are not paved with mosaics,

neither are its men and women angels. You cannot revolutionise it, so it is well to be content ;
though that young lady looks to me as though she
expected the new Ministry to resign at her bidding.'

'No,' said the Poetess, calmly, 'I do not ; and
neither am I, like Disraeli, "on the side of the
angels," but I think that the taint of worldliness
hinders many a soul in its upward progress. The
streets of the world may not be paved with mosaics,
but surely one may aim at an individual purity that
shall bear the test of pearl.'

'Ah !' said Lady Charlecote, rising somewhat
suddenly, 'I know the very man for you. He has
just your ideas. I met him at a dinner party the
other night, and he talked like a book for an hour
without ceasing. You shall meet him at my house.
Now, my dears, I shall expect you on Thursday.
Can't manage it ? Well, then, on the next Thursday. You must positively come then ; I have a
reception in honour of my niece—just married, you
know, to a young barrister. I shall be able to get
you plenty of invitations afterwards, I daresay—
yes, yes, I know—afterwards. Good-bye, my dears.
Come and see me when you want cheering up. I
like young people ; they refresh me. Good-bye.'

It was characteristic of the two girls that they
looked with different eyes upon the prospect thus
opened out before them.

'What are you thinking, Poetess?' said Sybil, as
she looked up at the grave, somewhat troubled, face
of her friend. 'Do you not feel elated at the idea
of the reception, and the crowd, and the charming
young men?'

She spoke jestingly; her gay humour perceived
the element of drollery in the contrasts of the
scene.

But Michal gave an impatient sigh.

'Sybil,' she said abruptly, 'it is of no use. I
shall never understand these people; never like
them. We belong to different worlds; we do not
even speak the same language. There is no
sympathy between us, no accord; their life would
be to me as terrible as the Mediæval hell. "Life,"
did I say? It is not life; it is in correspondence
only with a fragment of their environment, and
that most sordid and mean. They will worship
their false gods to the end, and will force others to
worship them; but they shall not force *me*. They
will drink to the full of the cup of their falsehood
and littleness, and force it upon others; but they
shall not poison *me*.'

Sybil listened to the passionate outburst in
silence. She knew Michal's intense hatred of
shams and narrow ideals, and she expected this
reaction.

'A second sage of Chelsea has arisen,' she said,

smiling, ' to hurl anathemas upon an indignant and scornful people. My Poetess, you are right, I am certain. My sympathies, as you know, are yours ; but I think that there is a time to speak and a time to be silent.'

'No one will be likely to call such a platitude in question,' said Michal, half jestingly. 'Go on ; paraphrase if you will.'

'I mean,' said Sybil, knitting her brows in an intense effort at lucidity, 'that it is of no earthly use for you to bring your lofty ideals into contact with the fashionable world. I know you; I know that it will be very hard for you in many cases to resist from speaking your mind, and speaking it boldly; but, my Poetess, consider. What is it to them that we esteem them poor instead of rich?— that we do not consider a wealthy marriage the ' be all and end all ' of existence?—that we do not desire the patronage of titles?—and that our lives have other aims and ambitions? Darling, they would not understand us, all this would be as so much Sanskrit in their ears. *Vox populi* is *vox Dei* in the fashionable world of London.'

There was a long pause.

'You remind me of a quotation in my book of extracts,' said Michal at length, with a smile

'Fain would I something say, but to what end ?
Thou hast nor soul nor ears to apprehend.'

'I will think over what you say, *cara mia.* You may be right, and self-repression is as much a duty as honesty of speech. The difficulty is to obtain a right estimate of such virtue in its proportion to the rest of our lives.'

Sybil saw that the grave face was still troubled. The Poetess did not take life easily; its problems were very real to her, its mysteries very deep; *Ernst ist das Leben* was the watchword constantly before her eyes, and the plexus of conflicting tendencies around her served to intensify its meaning.

The lighter-hearted Sybil, who herself was troubled by no psychological speculations, nevertheless knew the moods of her friend, and the love in her taught her sympathy.

She laid her auburn curls caressingly on Michal's shoulder with the confidence of a child who knows its power.

The dark eyes immediately softened.

'We won't go oftener to these receptions, my Poetess,' said Sybil gently, 'than we can possibly, help. That will be one way out of our difficulties.'

'I hope so,' said Michal with a smile.

CHAPTER VI.

'But I, who am of lighter mood, will laugh.'—BYRON.'

THE next caller came on a bright afternoon in June. The trim housemaid, looking up from the pantry window, caught a glimpse of a gentleman in a velvet jacket; she noticed that he also carried a large and curiously-fashioned cane.

'Is Miss Murray at home?' inquired the visitor.

'No, sir, both ladies are out; they will be home to tea.'

'I will wait,' said the visitor, and he walked in.

The housemaid opened the door of the larger sitting-room and closed it upon the gentleman.

'Emily,' said an uncertain voice softly from the top of the staircase.

The girl paused and looked up. Miss Sally had just issued from one of the upper rooms in time to catch a glimpse of the visitor and his cane. She knew that her boarders were both absent, and her gentle heart misgave her as to the propriety of allowing a strange man to enter. So few strange men ever entered her respectable dwelling; she did not wish that they should enter. Her experience had led her to walk warily wherever they were concerned.

'Is that a gentleman to see the young ladies?' she asked in a whisper, descending slowly and with caution, one step at a time.

'Yes, ma'am.'

A bright thought struck the old lady.

'Has he a black bag, Emily?' she asked.

'No, ma'am, no bag at all.'

'Then he can't be the piano-tuner. Dear me, what is to be done?'

The girl, unable to understand the difficulty, retired, and Miss Sally, wavering between curiosity and fear, descended the staircase noiselessly, until she came within sight of the inner room. The door that was nearest to her was open, so were the folding-doors inside.

The strange man had wandered through into the smaller room, and stood with his back to her.

'Merciful heavens! he is a thief and is going to steal,' she said to herself, descending another step, her fear getting the better of her timidity.

Then a movement on the part of the stranger set her fears at rest. He was holding a cabinet photo in his hand, and gazing at it earnestly. The little mistress of the house turned and ascended the staircase, her respectable old face wrinkled into a smile. He was neither a piano-tuner nor a thief, she said to herself shrewdly ; he was a lover, that was certain. She knew it by the rapt expression of his face as he looked at the photo. How much longer would he have stood there? she wondered. The calm pulsation of her heart increased perceptibly in speed as she thought of it : she wished she had waited to see.

Meanwhile, Leslie Vernon was bestowing a critical analysis upon the portrait, which was a tolerably faithful representation of Sybil. It did not please him ; it wanted warmth and colour—the red of the lips and the hair's sweet gold. He turned from it to the wider contemplation of the room and its contents. The light from the window was good. He glanced outside upon the square enclosure of turf that serves as a typical London garden, and he marvelled at the bright array of summer flowers which bloomed from their earthy beds. Someone cared for those dwarf roses and pansies and pinks, he thought with satisfaction. Sybil's easel stood by the window, but there were no studies visible. The large bookcase was opposite, and the oaken escritoire in a corner. His appreciative eye rested now upon the many Oriental knick-knacks and curios, now upon the array of books. These interested him ; he examined them more closely.

The monuments of ancient genius held an honoured place; the philosophy and the poetry of all ages stood side by side, and the modern world followed closely in the wake with honourable and honoured names. The artist glanced from Plato to John Stuart Mill with scant appreciation. 'Omnivorous, indeed,' he said to himself. Then he spied the *Magazine of Art*, and smiled. It was a trace of Sybil.

Presently he became aware of a quiet footstep, and he awoke from his reverie to greet the Poetess.

'Sybil will be home from the studio shortly,' she said, intercepting his apology. 'I have been at the Cromwell Road Museum all day. You were right to come in. I see that you have found food convenient for you.'

'Food,' he echoed grimly, with a comic side glance at the bookcase.

'Yes, there is food enough to keep all the readers in England for a month.'

'Have you honestly read all those books once through?'

The Poetess looked at him with her grave smile.

'I believe I have, but do you not realise that a library is like a large encyclopædia; it is for reference. The art of reading even, sometimes, may consist in knowing how to skip judiciously. But I think I may say of most of my volumes that they are my friends, and require no such treatment. Will you come into the other room? It is more spacious than this, which is our workshop.'

'So I suppose,' replied Leslie Vernon, as he sank comfortably into an easy chair, and watched the sweep of Michal's skirt as she stood over the tea-table.

'So you are happy here?' he said, abruptly, not raising his eyes from the gleaming eyes of the tiger whose beautiful skin lay stretched out under his feet.

'Yes,' said Michal, slowly, 'we are very happy.'

'And she—Miss Murray—is content with her work?'

Michal smiled.

'You, of all men, should know that content is not the frame of mind most characteristic of earnest workers. But she has perseverance and enthusiasm to back her.'

The artist smiled bitterly.

'Ah! enthusiasm! Yes, they all have when they start. They soon leave *that* behind them in the struggle.'

Michal came and stood before him. He looked up from the gleaming eyes of the tiger, and met her earnest gaze.

'It is those who throw it away who lose the race,' she said quietly.

'I daresay,' he answered, with a careless gesture.

'You speak from a woman's standpoint. Women are more personal and enthusiastic than men, and some of you are so terribly in earnest. It is not worth while.'

There was a sudden rush and bustle, and Sybil entered like a breezy gust of southern wind.

The artist greeted her with a smile, noticing, as he did so, a shade of weariness in the bright young eyes.

'You have kept your friend waiting for tea,' he said gravely. 'What apologies can you offer?'

'None,' was the cheery answer, as Sybil revealed a mass of tumbled, auburn hair from under her large black hat. 'I have kept you waiting also, I am afraid, Mr Vernon.'

The artist sat back in his chair, and stared again at the tiger. He was trying to frame some excuse for his visit, but his voice refused to utter any. He took the cup from Sybil's hand with a strong feeling of embarrassment, and she noticed the reflection of it in his eyes.

'Do you like tea?' she said slowly.

'Yes,' he answered with a short, spontaneous laugh. 'I was only thinking how seldom I took a cup from a woman's hand, that was all.'

'I suppose that is your own fault,' said the Poetess gently, 'or your own pleasure.'

'It depends,' he answered. 'I care little for the

world, and it dislikes me. So I stay at home with my pipe and my misanthropy.'

'And your Art,' hazarded Sybil.

'Art!' His cynicism grated on her ear. 'Capacity for earning bread and cheese! I am too old to sit and make idealistic theories about Art. Enthusiasm and ideals are for the young. I have outgrown them.'

Sybil grew depressed, and made no answer. She knew that he could not be much more than forty, yet he talked like a man whose days are ended.

'That is your misfortune,' said the Poetess, with flashing eyes.

'Undoubtedly. It is the misfortune of most people who blunder through the world, expecting all manner of blessings and happiness, and find that the game is not worth the candle.'

There was a pause. Rifts of sunshine, flickering through the open window, lost themselves in the meshes of Sybil's hair. Leslie Vernon looked from her graceful head to the black coronet of the Poetess. He did not stop to analyse his appreciation of the whole scene; he only knew that it was infinitely restful to him—infinitely sweet.

After tea was over, the conversation drifted easily into idle channels. The artist drew from Sybil some further details respecting her studio work and the general ordering of their lives.

D

'We play also,' said she brightly. 'In the evening we have our music and work and gardening, and Michal reads aloud. Sometimes we go to St James's Hall for a concert.'

'Ah! then the roses and pansies out there owe their beauty to your culture,' said Leslie Vernon. 'That accounts for it. And you haunt the Cromwell Road Museum, Miss Iliff? What do you do there all day? Meditate, I suppose, under the ribs of the giant elephants, or make studies of the Malayan skull?'

'Neither,' said Michal tranquilly. 'But there are many attractions. There is the mineral room and the botanical—both charming. There are the birds, dumb, alas! and stationary, but still beautiful, and the central gallery alone is a famous hunting-ground for a student.'

'It is a glorious place,' said Sybil, emphatically.

The artist meditated.

'You embrace a large circle,' he said, after a pause. 'I should have thought that such diversity of attainment might tend rather to diffuseness than harmony. Pardon me—I know, of course, that you have the aspirations of a poet in your nature. Do you not think that in your case, as perhaps in Browning's, a too extensive knowledge might prove a stumbling block in Art?'

'I do not think that is sufficient to account for

Browning's peculiarities,' said Sybil. 'It is his style, surely, that mars the beauty of many thoughts.'

Michal was silent for a space, and when she spoke a wave of colour swept her olive cheek, leaving it very pale.

'I think you lower the function of a poet,' she said slowly. 'You do not realise that he should be seer and interpreter as well as singer of sweet songs. Poetry should be the interpretation of life —the expression of all that is noblest, and to see and to express needs rare culture, rare knowledge— " tilling the old world's wisdom till it grow a garden for the wandering of our feet." Then, with breadth of knowledge comes breadth of thought, greater love, deeper sympathy ; and when, like Cædmon, we " sing of things created," our songs shall gladden and refresh the hearts of men. Thus, I take it, no knowledge can come amiss to us ; no interests, however varied, can be lost.'

'You have a high standard,' said the artist gravely.

'We want the highest standards now,' she answered, 'and the best in Art.'

Again silence, and Sybil, knowing that the Poetess did not speak without an effort of the things that were most sacred to her, changed the current of their talk.

'Do you know,' she cried suddenly, 'that we have already made up our minds for a holiday? You may think it weakness on our part, but our longing for wild roses and the honeysuckle has grown too intense to be withstood. We are country girls, you see, and this new element of bricks and pavement is a little trying at first.'

'Ah! I wondered what the tiredness in your eyes might mean,' said the artist quietly, 'and I can sympathise. Where, then, do you propose to go?'

'We can always go when we like to a dear old friend at Haresfield,' answered Sybil. 'That is our old home, you know, and this lady was one of my father's oldest friends. I think the change will be good for us both.'

'Very good; and you can turn your attention to landscape sketching. If you are ever in need of a friendly criticism, I hope you will not scruple to let me help you if I can.'

Sybil's fair face grew warmer.

'I think you are very kind,' she said.

He rose from his chair as he answered:

'No, I only please myself, and mine are purely selfish motives. In the meanwhile, I had forgotten what is a rarity in my life—I have an engagement this evening.'

The girls rose also.

'I am going to the house of the only man in London whom I call friend.'

'Indeed! who is it?' asked Sybil, somewhat ashamed of her curiosity, which she was, nevertheless, unable to restrain.

'Lord Trevelyan. If you are in the habit of following the political currents of the day, his name will be familiar to you.'

'Certainly; the most bigoted Conservative in the House of Lords,' said the Poetess sharply.

'Ah! your bitterness betrays a revolutionary instinct,' said the artist. 'Yet you have taken a fairly accurate measure of my friend. He is every inch an English aristocrat, born to the purple. He lives on the lands that have been his ancestors' for generations. He has Plantagenet blood in his veins, and he cannot forget that fact. Yet, in spite of it all, I like Trevelyan. He is haughty and unbending to the world, but not to me; and the world is as wearisome a treadmill to him as it is to myself.'

Sybil was interested. Michal received the explanation in unsympathetic silence. She knew that Lord Trevelyan was an enemy to progress, as she understood it; that he opposed the spasmodic movements set on foot, at intervals, in the cause of women, by the more liberal-hearted of the community, and the sentiment of abstract justice was a strong passion with the Poetess.

'It is a pity that your friend does not use his influence in a less contracted circle,' she said coldly.

'I agree with you,' replied Leslie Vernon, with quick emphasis. 'It is a pity; but it is the inevitable result of his heredity and the associations of his life; such surroundings are paralysing to most men. But, at any rate, I must away. I thank you for your gracious reception of a vagabond.'

The Poetess smiled faintly. Sybil made cheery answer,—

'I think the debt is on our side. I am sure we were very pleased to see you.'

The sweet eyes looked truthfully into his face for an instant, and again he yielded where he had meant to be strong.

'Then, perhaps, I will come again when you return from your visit,' he said gently. 'And you must always let me know if I can help you—in any way.'

And the door closed upon Leslie Vernon.

Sybil became suddenly aware of the earnest gaze of Michal bent upon her in scrutiny. Something in the intensity of the look made her wonder.

'What is it, Poetess?' she said, softly, drawing nearer to her friend; and then she gave a sudden dismayed interjection, for there were surely tears in the great, dark eyes.

'Nothing, dear, at all,' said Michal quickly. 'The sun was in my eyes.'

And she said to herself, bitterly, that it was the first time that she had yielded to the weakness of sheltering beneath a lie. She went into the garden with the pretext of watering the flowers, and she bent over the fragrant petals in anxious thought.

'Does he mean it?' she asked herself restlessly. 'Why does a man of his position live the life of a hermit, yet show himself so ready to help a young and pretty girl? Why is he so evidently attracted by her, and yet so restrained sometimes in manner? Is he in earnest, or is he playing?'

And the fire that leapt into her deep eyes at the thought might have made any man pause before entering in the lists against her.

'If he comes here to play the fool with her,' said the Poetess between her set teeth, 'he shall pay for it.'

Hers was not usually a suspicious nature, but her love for Sybil was all the stronger by reason of a certain protective element in it, and such love begets distrust.

Meanwhile, Sybil, the light-hearted, was singing in the parlour the refrain of an old-world song :—

'Then hey ! for boot and horse, lad,
And round the world away !
Young blood must have its course, lad,
And every dog his day.'

CHAPTER VII.

'Perfectly beautiful; let it be granted her; where is the fault?
Dead perfection, nothing more.'—TENNYSON.

'JOHN, you have been mooning over that paper for the last hour, and it is now four o'clock. You *must* go and dress. I have told you repeatedly that I have a reception to-day, and there you are, still in your carpet slippers.'

Sir John Charlecote looked up with a pained expression at the face of his wife. He took up his cigar and his paper, and prepared for instant flight. He never made the least resistance to the demands of his spirited partner, partly because he was not capable of showing a lengthened resistance to her concentrated energies. She was a most wonderful woman, he thought, patiently. He listened sometimes with a feeling of positive awe to her neatly-made matrimonial schemes, her marvellous stories, —all culled from the 'best authorities'—her inti-

56

mate acquaintance with the Court and Ministerial details, which had been gathered at the Embassy Ball.

He listened and marvelled. He knew that he was but a dull-brained individual, and was content to admire his wife in silence, and when the rattle of their social environment became too much for him, he retired to the Athenæum and found peace. The receptions bored him perhaps more than any other form of entertainment, but Lady Charlecote would have him to appear, and he surrendered with the meekness habitual to him, and moved about among the guests with a gentle, if somewhat con-strained, courtesy.

He wondered sometimes what was the use of it all; it seemed to him passing strange that so many intelligent human beings should care for the crowd and exertion and empty tittle-tattle which made up the sum of this so-called social life. He was too paralysed by Custom to show open resentment, but in secret he wondered and sighed.

'Sybil Murray is coming this afternoon,' said Lady Charlecote, as she entered the drawing-room briskly, and found her husband thoughtfully sur-veying the grotesque perfection of his clothes. 'And Michal Iliff—you know poor Frank's ward—the girl he picked up somewhere: no one knows who she is, but she has a splendid figure and a most aristocratic head. They are taking girls, both of them, poor things.'

Why "poor things" if they are so fascinating?' hazarded Sir John.

'Because it is of no use for a girl to be taking unless there is somebody to see her? How dull you are, John! I told you that they are living together in an out-of-the-way part of London' (the speaker was apt to be vague as to locality), 'and how they are to meet any men, unless they come to my house, I fail to see. But no doubt I shall often ask them.'

'Yes,' said Sir John, absently.

He had no doubt whatever that the girls would gladly avail themselves of the proffered hospitality; all the girls of his acquaintance did so, and he had seldom met any woman of an unusual type. Such is the fatal influence of a system which has set up its own petty standards of Custom and prejudice against the divine spark of individual liberty that should exist in every human soul. God's seal becomes obliterated, individuality merged in the conventional type of social servitude.

Lady Charlecote was essentially a good-natured woman; she would do anyone a kindness if it lay within her power to do so, and this trait made her deservedly a favourite in her extensive coterie.

Sir John watched her as she moved about the

drawing-room with an air of accelerated energy, and thought, as usual, what a wonderful woman she was. The reception to-day was especially crowded. Michal, after it was over, could conjure up only a vague remembrance of coffee, sweetmeats and flowers, and of three hundred people who talked incessantly, and who filled the rooms, the hall, and the stairs.

Sybil's less dreamy observation furnished her with many details that the Poetess failed to detect. There was one particular incident that remained in her memory. She had been talking to a youth to whom the kindly hostess had introduced her, and the conversation, not too animated at its best, had slackened painfully; it was therefore no dis-appointment to her when the young man was sucked into the vortex of the crowd, and she was left to follow her own thoughts and to listen to a brilliant rendering of Paderewski.

She was quite at her ease in the kaleidoscopic scene around her, and whereas Michal found therein only food for grave reflection, she divined the lighter current of humour that would make itself apparent here and there.

Presently she became aware of a tall man stand-ing near her, who was looking about him with a grave and hesitating air. The lady with whom he had been speaking was forced to turn away in re-

sponse to other claims, and he, left for the moment
without any special duty to perform, caught Sybil's
amused glance, and smiled back involuntarily into
the candid eyes. She seemed to him very fresh
and very pretty. He came nearer and spoke in a
low tone.

'Do you—do you enjoy this?' he asked hesitatingly, as though fearful of being overheard.

Sybil recognised her host and smiled.

'It is meant to be enjoyed, is it not?' she
answered with naïve simplicity.

Sir John came a little nearer; a sudden access
of confidential frankness conquered his natural
reserve.

'I think it's a terrible bore,' he said with grave
and intense emphasis, and Sybil's amusement grew.

'Then why do you entertain in this manner?'
was her not unnatural question.

'Everybody does it,' said Sir John.

Here was no possibility of argument; he had
struck the false keynote of that inharmonious
structure of which he was content to play so insig-
nificant a part. The music of Orpheus can awake
in us no harmony if our souls be out of tune.

Meanwhile, the Poetess, after drifting hither and
thither aimlessly, and having begun several con-
versations which ended in sudden annihilation,
found herself peaceably anchored by the piano,

listening with genuine pleasure to the fragments of excellent music and recitation which were provided from time to time.

There was a lull in the babel of conversation as the first notes of one of Rubenstein's sweetest melodies floated out into the room. It was greeted with a hum of appreciation, and Michal's enjoyment found spontaneous utterance in a few warm words of praise.

'Yes, of course, it is a rare perfection,' said a clear voice at her side. 'But you would not tolerate dilletantism in that class of people. They are paid for their services, and they do our pleasure.

The voice flowed smoothly in its perfect intonation—clear, exact and cold. Michal turned quickly to look at the speaker, and having once done so, she could not withdraw her gaze, for the woman whom she saw was beautiful.

She wore an exquisite gown of soft copper-coloured silk, with blue embroideries, her gleaming hair showed the varying tints of oak leaves that are clothed in autumnal gold; her eyes were an indescribable colour—in some lights blue, in others black; the expression that dwelt upon her perfect features was one of unalterable coldness and hauteur; it was as though Nature had produced a marvellous imitation—a likeness which should resemble the human form in all its loveliness, and yet be without a soul.

Each movement of the beautiful figure proclaimed its aristocratic culture; the blue blood might be traced in every vein.

'Who is that lady?' asked Michal of a young girl who sat in her vicinity.

'That is Lady Trevelyan,' was the answer, given in a somewhat surprised tone.

'She is very beautiful,' said the Poetess involuntarily, as she watched the queenly form pass from her horizon.

'Beautiful! Yes, she has been one of the Court beauties for many seasons, you know, and she still preserves her reputation in spite of many lovely debutantes who are presented every year. She has no troubles, I suppose, and that may be the secret. At any rate, she never shows any feeling of any kind; she is always the same, perfectly correct and perfectly charming.'

The Poetess mused. Her southern blood rose in revolt against an impenetrable human wall. She did not believe in such a structure; she could not respect it. Intense natures need a corresponding warmth; the ice of an unbroken equanimity freezes an ardent soul.

Later, when at last the crowd gave way a little, and Sybil and the Poetess, inconspicuous fragments of the great kaleidoscope, drifted out of the brilliant gathering into the still, June air, Michal said meditatively,—

'I have seen to-day, *cara mia*, the loveliest human shell in the world, only it was empty.'

'How do you mean?'

'I mean that the workmanship was exquisite—a miracle of design—but the animating principle, the life that should have shone in the deeps of those wonderful eyes, was absent, and left no trace. But oh! the design and the beauty!'

'You mean Lady Trevelyan,' said Sybil quickly. 'Yes; what a wonderful piece of crystallised perfection, isn't she? I don't know why, but it made me think of Guinevere. "Oh! imperial moulded form, and beauty such as never woman wore!"'

Michal shook her head.

'I cannot imagine the existence of an aberrant love seeking "a smaller soul, Lancelot or another," under that marble covering. But we may misjudge her after all.'

'I wonder what Leslie Vernon thinks,' said Sybil: 'he never mentioned her.'

'We will ask him,' said the Poetess.

CHAPTER VIII.

'Great, consistent ; wearing all that weight of learning
lightly like a flower.'—TENNYSON.

THE afternoon class in Raffini's studio was over,
and a general turmoil of change and movement
began to manifest itself throughout the rooms.
The students, each dominated by an earnest desire
for individual cleanliness, worked feverishly to that
end with palette-knives and turpentine ; the odour
of soap and water mingled agreeably with the other
perfumes especially characteristic of the artistic
coterie, while the hum of cheery voices, occasional
splash of water, and the rattle of paints and brushes
made the accustomed music of the hour.

Sybil had just returned into the studio, and was
standing idly by the mantelpiece, regardless of the
fact that a long line of dust and a patch of yellow
ochre were leaving a badge of the profession upon
the sleeve of her black gown.

She was toying with her brushes in a desultory

way, and she was very tired. The unaccustomed monotony of conscientious work was telling upon her none too powerful physique, and in the golden-brown eyes there dwelt that look of weariness which betrays the ardent but tired spirit of a worker who needs repose.

But Sybil was first a woman, then an artist. There was no glowing genius striving within her to burst its prison-bars; none of the boundless ambition which, in the proud consciousness of innate power, soars continually beyond the earthly limits of its activity. She was able to turn her mind from the introspective analysis which is inseparable from such ambitions, to the idle contemplation of the world in which she dwelt, and this capacity saved her from much *ennui.* She was listening now with some slight interest to the art *patois* of two young students who were discussing the delicacy of Rubens and the vigour of Michael Angelo with an insight that would have surprised both masters had they but been able to profit by such criticism.

The studio was nearly empty, and rough attempts at an elementary tidiness had given its picturesque details a somewhat depressed air. At least, so Sybil thought, as she looked round with the genial eye of the Bohemian upon a scene which, to a more correctly-trained intelligence, might have

E

appeared barbaric; but her wandering gaze was arrested by a woman.

There was nothing unusual in the appearance of a model at this hour; such often came and were interviewed. But there was something in the face of the woman that appealed strangely to Sybil's imagination. She became possessed by an unconquerable conviction that she had seen the woman before.

But where? Her memory was silent. The model was of Southern type; she wore a somewhat faded gown, with spotless kerchief folded about her bosom. She had a wedding-ring upon her finger, and ear-rings in her ears. She held her head high, and gazed with apparently inconsequent defiance at every stranger. Her eyes were very dark, and gleamed in their sockets like danger-signals; the fire of youth had been, as one might conjecture, all too roughly extinguished, and only a smouldering heap of passions lay dormant there. Woe to him who should strike a match in their vicinity!

It was with an effort that Sybil at last turned away; and in the omnibus that bore her homewards, her mind still hovered about the memory of those passionate eyes, wondering why they should seem so familiar.

Her head was aching, and the uncertain movement of the omnibus did not tend to relieve the pain. She alighted therefore in the Edgware Road, and pursued her way tranquilly homewards, unconscious of the keen scrutiny of two restless eyes.

Leslie Vernon, who was walking on the other side of the road, noted, with the quick observation peculiar to him, the slight droop of Sybil's head and the want of elasticity in her movements.

'She is over-working,' he said to himself; and the suggestion annoyed him strangely.

He crossed the road, and overtook her in a few long, easy strides.

Sybil greeted him with her usual fearless cordiality as he walked on by her side.

'You are tired,' he said abruptly, ignoring the simple comments which she strung together as a prelude to conversation. 'You are abominably tired.'

Physical weakness was Sybil's *bête noir*, and, as such, she would never own its existence willingly; but to-day her common sense warned her that denial would be useless, so she said, with a little laugh,—

'That is no irremediable evil. It is rather the satisfaction of the worker who feels that he has justified himself—I mean, his existence.'

'It is the penalty of *over*-work,' said the artist sharply, ignoring her lame phrase. 'Do you think

I don't know what it means? When I started in life as a boy, with all your pluck and twice your strength, do you think I found my level without toiling for it? For some years, I can tell you, I worked myself nearly to death, as you are about to do, for I had very little money to back me, and few friends. The money has come since, of course, and the name —but the friends—' he laughed bitterly. 'Never mind, that was my own fault. But with you there is no excuse for all this feverish activity. You can afford to wait; and you are a woman, and have less strength for the conflict.'

'I know,' said Sybil simply. 'That is one of the greatest mysteries in life to me. *Why* should we be less strong?'

He laughed again with the same ring of cynicism.

'Don't come to me for solutions of the enigmas of life,' he flung back hastily. 'I have drifted long since into the abyss of the "Everlasting No," as our dyspeptic friend has aptly termed the pessimistic view of the universe. It is a world of unsolved riddles; and, for my own part, I wonder often at the long endurance of women. I suppose the reason of their patience is that so few of them ever think. If they did rouse themselves to think at all, the crusade against injustice would be waged more successfully in savage and civilised lands.'

Sybil looked at him with interest.

'Some of them *are* thinking nowadays,' she answered, 'and acting also. If you believe at all in evolution, you can hardly overlook a change that is manifesting itself in so many ways. You must recognise the landmarks slowly but surely planted in the sands of time; and, for my own part, I cannot but believe always that the changes will work for good.'

'If the changes are to aid in the annihilation of the prejudices by which women are handicapped, I agree with you entirely. But social evolution seems to me a phrase for a remarkably slow process, rendered slower by men's prejudice. You are an optimist, of course, because you are young.'

'I am an optimist,' said Sybil simply, 'because I believe in love. Love seems to me the great panacea. It does not make unjust things right, but it softens the injustice. It hallows relationships which would otherwise be unendurable; it is our great compensation, and makes us content to wait.'

He looked at her, and saw the sweet eyes shining with a tenderness and meaning before which his own glance fell.

'You take a more contented view of things than your Poetess,' he said. 'Where is she, by-the-bye? I do not really think that it is safe for her to go out alone; you will lose her one of these days.'

He sought to conceal the emotion which had moved him under a bantering tone. Sybil looked at him in amaze.

'What can you mean? Lose the Poetess?'

'I mean that she will probably be run over or robbed,' said the artist, with a sharp curve at the corners of his mouth, betokening grim amusement. 'I saw her the other day in Edgware Road, going dreaming along, with a mind so evidently abstracted from all worldly matters that the passers-by glanced at her and smiled. She was carrying a paper bag too, from which fell an occasional shrimp. I imagine that she was holding it sideways, and I daresay by the time she reached home there were no shrimps left, only a bag with an appetising odour. It afforded me quite ten minutes' amusement as I walked behind her, I can assure you.'

Sybil was laughing heartily.

'Poor dear Poetess! Just like her! I thought there seemed to be very few shrimps at tea that night. I remember it quite well, but then, you know, people always cheat Michal. She never finds it out, and she never knows whether her change is right or wrong. I never say anything about it to worry her, because she cannot help it, and really sometimes it is such fun. But this is my destination, Mr Vernon. You will come in and have tea with us?'

The artist hesitated, unwilling to say yes, unable to say no. It was the old story: prudence and inclination striving for the mastery, judgment and passion at war. Then he raised his eyes suddenly; meeting her smiling glance, he assented and followed her indoors.

Tea was ready, but Michal had not returned. Sybil looked round with a disappointed air.

'The Poetess is late to-day,' she said, 'but we will wait a little while, if you don't mind.'

Leslie Vernon rested in the easy chair, and looked down as usual at the tiger's gleaming eyes. The fragrance of rose petals hung lightly upon the atmosphere; it was all very peaceful, very sweet, and the artist strove with himself no longer: his soul rested in the quiet. Sybil sat opposite to him, and the talk ran easily over indifferent topics, while she, ever and anon, threw an expectant look towards the door.

'You leave your manuscripts in unguarded fashion,' said the artist, picking up a page of loose paper from the floor.

'Oh! that is only a piece from Michal's extract book,' replied Sybil. 'It is of no consequence, I expect, or she would have been more careful.'

He glanced at the hurried writing in pencil upon the sheet and read it over hastily at first, then again. He looked up in silence—an intense feeling robbed him of speech. It was as though a breath from another and more beautiful world had blown upon the ashes of his life—a creating, vivifying breath, and yet in all its beauty and heaven-born freshness dwelt something akin to pain.

'Beauty for ashes,' he said simply, as Sybil took the paper gently from him to investigate its contents.

Her eyes shone.

'The verses are not copied, I see,' she said smiling. 'They are hers.'

Unspeakable wonder kept the artist mute.

'I could not have believed it,' he replied after a pause. 'They are sublime in their restfulness and infinite simplicity. She is a genius, then!'

Sybil nodded gravely and put the paper away.

'I need not let her know that you have seen them. No one at present sees her work but myself.'

''To you are dedicated the first fruits,' said the artist. 'It is a pure gift and untainted. No work done in after years is like unto it, but all have not a shrine at which to lay their offerings. She is happy, little girl, in having you.'

Sybil looked up and saw the pain of an infinite regret in his deep eyes. They both fell into silence. Presently the door opened and Michal came towards them. Her greeting to the artist was but slight, and her glance rested inquiringly upon Sybil.

'All right, my Poetess,' said the latter brightly, flinging back a cheery challenge from her tired eyes. 'I am not at all over-worked, and I only want some tea. What makes you so late, dear?'

'I took the wrong omnibus,' said Michal composedly, 'and went on to Finchley. That was all.'

She went to the table and prepared for action. Sybil shook her head with a comic gesture of despair.

Leslie Vernon was still silent; his critical glance rested with a new attention upon the beautiful figure and earnest face of Michal. She was not looking at him : he thought he detected a certain restraint in her manner, but that might be only the accusing fancy of his own restlessness.

He thought of the little manuscript with the few sweet lines of verse, and he thought of the author as of a being somewhat removed from the practical world of men, and yet whose influence might dwell in her generation as a fragrant, God-given thing. He thought that the lines inspired by another friendship, not less true, might apply with fitness to Michal, and he found himself repeating them to himself dreamily,—

> 'And thou art worthy ; full of power ;
> As gentle ; liberal minded, great,
> Consistent ; wearing all that weight
> Of learning lightly like a flower.'

It was with an effort that he roused himself to

reply to the cheery tones of Sybil. Their talk,
fragmentary at first and disconnected, drifted soon
into personalities.

'When is your projected gambol coming off?
asked the artist genially.

'Next week,' said Sybil. 'I think we are like
school children anticipating their "treat": we can
hardly speak of anything else, Mr Vernon. Every
leaf brings a message from our old haunts, every
breath of wind seems to blow from the purple hills.
Perhaps we shall return better equipped for the
work-a-day world of London.'

A wistfulness had come into her eyes; she
seemed to be looking far ahead into the veiled unknown. Was she already regretting the plunge
into an artistic career, the artist wondered, or was
it only one of those phases of depression to which
the artistic temperament is subject? He glanced
again at the Poetess; her grave eyes were lowered.

' I suppose we cannot over-estimate the influence
of surroundings,' he said at length. 'To some there
is an incentive, even in the bustle and restlessness
of the great city: to others, the effect is diametri-
cally opposite. I think that your pining thus
for the country life proves you in need of rest.
Your spirit is not as yet entirely tutored to this
submission.'

'That is just it,' said Sybil thoughtfully. 'It

seems to me that, in all work, the training of the will should precede all other trainings.'

'Surely,' said the Poetess, 'the will can but work in unison with the faculties in the exercise of a beloved art.'

'I think you are mistaken,' said Leslie Vernon. 'The will must itself be educated—must itself become the central force that directs and controls, and its power is manifested in the unity of the results. An imperfect will begets dilletantism. Of course I know that I am skirting debatable ground, that I am speaking as if I assume beyond a doubt the freedom of the will, but in these cases I think we must argue as though we were indeed practically free. Without pretending to solve the riddle involved, we must limit ourselves to the practical issue in daily life. Art is a long discipline; the best years of a man's life are spent in the mastery of the technique; it would be strange if at last he did not possess, in some degree, the virtues of patience and humility.'

'I am glad you admit even an indirect good in the exercise of the artistic faculty,' said Michal, smiling.

'I *do* admit it. I say that it is an excellent training school. I never said that it was a paradise (unless of fools). I do not look upon the profession as a means of elevating the masses or even

one's own individual soul. I do not believe in pan-
aceas, but I do believe in the mental discipline
accruing from steady work.'

He spoke with a warmth unusual in him; the
interest of the discussion was felt by each of them
to be very real.

'Think of Mulready,' said the artist again, suddenly. 'You know that, before the execution of a
new picture, he prepared himself for it by a special
training—a special study of each separate part.
Think of the superb Leonardo! Here was a man
at once a civil engineer, an artist, a scientific dis-
coverer! Was such versatility, think you, ever
acquired without a corresponding toil? And even
he fell short of the highest artistic excellence; one
life could not maintain so many developments of
equal power.'

'He lived in an age specially favourable to him,'
said the Poetess. 'In these days I think that over-
production seems to be the greatest danger.'

'Not only in these days,' he interrupted her, 'but
always—in every life. Of course, it is especially
the curse of impecuniosity—the levelling of literature and the fine arts to a trade; but it besets all
of us, and if I might frankly advise Miss Murray,
I should say, use your month of relaxation as a
rest. Store up energy rather than dissipate what
you have already stored.'

The Poetess threw a smiling glance at Sybil, who shook her head doubtfully.

'I don't think I could help sketching a little,' she said with an apologetic air.

'Then make it as little as you can. Keep your mind cool and open to receive impressions. Go to Nature, "not as lord, but servant"—not even as interpreter—just watch her moods, and learn. I speak to you as to one who can afford to wait. Remember that, your highest privilege, and be thankful for it.'

'Poetess,' cried Sybil suddenly, 'will you undertake to see that this good advice is carried out?'

'That's right,' laughed the artist. 'Put yourself into the safe hands of Miss Iliff; it is a matter in which you might safely trust her judgment.'

Michal smiled without much mirth, not feeling very sanguine as to the effect of her influence, and knowing that opposition is borne more readily from a stranger than from those we love. Moreover, from her habitual scorn of trivialities, she was accustomed to yield to the more practical sense of Sybil.

The artist was looking at her and thinking still of the verses which her genius had inspired. He was thinking, too, of the odd contrasts that are seen in life, and wondering at the power of a friendship that could unite such different elements into so perfect a whole. The serenity of these two lives made him a little envious. What gladness might have crowned his own successes if only the love of a kindred soul had blessed him with its sympathy! He rose and held out his hand to Michal.

'I hope you will both benefit by your gambol,' he said gravely, looking with a new reverence into her dark eyes.

She gave him a pleasant smile.

'I will, at any rate, try to dissuade Sybil from following Goethe's maxim,' she answered. '*Wie das Gestirn, ohne hast, aber ohne rast.* There is a nucleus of truth in it, but it is apt to be misleading.'

'It is a case where the letter killeth,' said the artist as he took his leave.

CHAPTER IX.

'I stood and stand alone.'—BYRON.

LESLIE VERNON walked slowly along the well-known thoroughfares now cleared of the ordinary traffic of the day. He turned in at the door of a pretty house in one of the quieter roads—a house of neat but somewhat cheerless aspect, with irreproachable curtains and blinds. The servants in that house were admirable; they served an easy master, and they were interfered with by no one, so that most of the rooms exhibited an unimpeachable propriety; the studio alone was exempt from the general rule. Here the artist worked, meditated, and smoked at his ease. It was a spacious dwelling, flooded with all the light obtainable from the two large windows in the northern wall. A few pictures broke the monotony of the other walls; statues, statuettes, a frieze from the Parthenon, and one or two beautiful capitals of the Corinthian

79

school served for ornament. The rest was entirely
plain.

A small flight of steps near the fireplace led to a
little gallery which encircled the upper part of the
room, at one end of which was a door leading into
a smaller apartment. This was a sort of accessory
workshop, a chaos of artistic lumber—open to the
owner alone. Leslie Vernon was known among
his brother artists as a recluse, and one, moreover,
with whom it might be dangerous to interfere.
He had no friends among them, and none ever
came to his studio in twilight hours to smoke and
chat over the events of the century. It was at
once his fault and his misfortune that the world
saw generally his least attractive side. Morose-
ness, cynicism, were his habitual weapons, and, as
usual, they turned against himself.

Of the kind heart and the strong human sympathy that lay crushed under the weight of a disappointed life, no one knew much. There were
one or two poor struggling artists whom he had
helped out of the mire of wretchedness and depression, but these, even whilst acknowledging their
debt to him, nevertheless stood somewhat in awe
of their benefactor. There were models, too, who
remembered many a kindness received from the
strange, solitary man ; and there were beggars who
knew that at his door, at least, they were sure of

obtaining some merited or unmerited favour. But to none of these was the real nature of the man revealed.

Grimly he had suffered in silence and alone. His friendship with Lord Trevelyan was a *camaraderie*, founded upon the mutual liking of two Englishmen frank enough to discuss the ordinary interests of their lives, and to find a pleasure in so doing, but who retained, nevertheless, a secret chamber in their consciousness locked to all the world. Neither was the balance exactly even. Leslie Vernon knew more of the weary nobleman than the latter knew of him, and the artist was content that it should be so.

It was sunset as he re-entered his studio that afternoon; a flush of dying carmine swept the heavens from the western horizon, floating little roseate trails of glory upward across the blue. Some of these sailed away on a northern voyage, growing ever smaller or less carmine, and the artist stood at his window to watch them on their way.

'They are like human souls,' he said to himself wearily. 'They start endowed with beauty and freshness, and float out into the great world in the first blush of their purity, and gradually they lose it all;—lose it by assimilation to their environment, and are at last undistinguished from the mass.'

F

He mused awhile in silence.   Fragments of
roseate cloud sailed past like little fairy cars upon
the ocean of infinity.   The poet's words were recalled to him,—

'In trailing clouds of glory do we come from
God, Who is our home,' he repeated slowly.
'Beautiful words, but of a dreamer—words such
as Michal Iliff might have uttered.   Yes, the
world is very beautiful for some people—for poets
and dreamers.   They live in "clouds of glory," but
who, unless they sleep, could dream the old dreams
now?'

He turned away abruptly.   An alien thought had
struck him; he tried to shake it off, and at that
moment the studio door opened to admit a tall,
erect man.

'Lord Trevelyan,' exclaimed the artist.   'This
is an unexpected pleasure.'

'To myself—Yes,' replied the Earl genially.
'I have escaped from the world for five minutes,
and have come to spend the interval peacefully on
your classic ground.'

'Good! take a chair—look out for the Aphrodite;
she is just behind you.'

'Aphrodite!' echoed the nobleman with a laugh.
'The very name proclaims one's emancipation.
I shall return refreshed to the atmosphere of
Gladyses and Elviras.'

The artist surveyed his guest critically. He saw a man of handsome features, with a stern mouth and weary eyes; a man who gave you the impression of being hurried, and sometimes overworked, albeit the possessor of a powerful and controlling will.

'So you are also *ennuyé?*' said Leslie Vernon with a short laugh. 'Has the enigma of this unintelligible world disturbed your conservative repose?'

The Earl smiled faintly.

'I do not come to you for a solution of the riddle of existence. I come to you for relaxation. My dear fellow, the world is growing too analytical by half: we analyse our motives and our thoughts and our convictions till the lunatic asylum opens its gates to receive our shattered nerves. For heaven's sake, let us cease for once from metaphysical speculation!'

'By all means. We will talk platitudes, and I will keep my reflections to myself. It does me good to know that Lord Trevelyan, the much-honoured star of political and social circles, seeks relaxation in the studio of a vagabond. Upon my word, it does me good. The contrasts of life are in themselves a study.'

'I should say that the retreat of a Diogenes would be a more significant appellation for your *intérieur,*' said the Earl drily. 'You are the most confoundedly cynical fellow I know.' He rose and walked up to the easel. 'Haven't you the ghost of a picture anywhere? Is there nothing but blank canvas? Ah! what's this?'

He had found a few water-colour sketches, and, amongst them, a rough study of a girl's head, which last he examined critically. The artist's brow contracted on a sudden, but he made no sign.

'Pretty little saucy face with the hazel eyes—what's all this German? Really, Vernon, you are growing remarkably poetical—" *Sie hat die goldenen Augen des Waldes Königin.*" Humph—a suggestion for your next picture, I suppose?'

'No; merely a sketch from memory.'

'Of a model?'

'No.'

With the quick intuition of good breeding, the Earl detected a restraint in his friend's manner and was silent.

'It is a sketch of Miss Murray,' said the artist, ashamed of his abruptness.

'Oh!'

The interjection was one of polite indifference. The Earl proceeded to examine the few other drawings that were at hand, commented upon them with considerable artistic insight, and then returned quietly to his chair.

CHAPTER X.

'Finding the middle or the mean in each case is a hard thing, just as finding the middle or centre of a circle is a thing that is not within the power of everybody, but only of him who has the requisite knowledge.'

Ethics of ARISTOTLE.

'WELL, I have only a few minutes' grace, as I said before,' remarked the Earl presently. 'There is a dinner at Greville's to-night, and I must look in afterwards at a meeting in Crossley Hall.'

'Primrose League?' said the artist smiling.

'No; but I have to speak; will you come?'

'What, and worship in the house of Rimmon? No, thank you.'

'Pshaw! my dear Vernon, you take life too seriously. The presence of a man at a political meeting does not compromise him, though, of course, I was only in joke.'

'Just so! I have, as you know, no fancy for bread-and-butter speeches—stump oratory in fact —and half truths. It is time that such should be no longer tolerated by reasonable beings. What

has Conservatism ever done for this world, I ask
you?'

'More good than revolutionary clap-trap,' responded the Earl gravely. 'The one is backed at
least by prudence and reserve, the other would land
a helpless people in anarchy aud confusion.'

'Well—then our unfortunate successors may find
confusion worse confounded', said the artist tranquilly; 'that's all. But you come here for relaxation, my lord, not for fruitless argument. How is
Lady Trevelyan?'

'I believe she is *in statu quo*, thank you. She
was lunching at the Embassy to-day, and I suppose we shall meet at dinner.'

'What would become of civilisation without its
meals?' said the artist, breaking into one of his
most spontaneous smiles.

'I suppose that married people would rarely
meet,' replied Lord Trevelyan carelessly, 'and the
business of life would be an even greater *corvée*
than it already is.'

The artist was silent, and after a pause the
conversation wandered, by mutual consent, into a
different channel until the Earl rose with a
sigh.

'If you walk, I will accompany you,' said
Leslie Vernon, 'but it is a dark evening and for-
bodes rain.'

'No matter; I like a walk as a relief from carriage exercise.'

So they went out together.

Deep twilight lay upon the city, and the lamps were lighted everywhere along the busy streets. The two men walked quickly, engrossed in conversation, noticing little of what they passed. As they neared Trafalgar Square, a woman walked past them in the opposite direction, and she threw a searching glance upon the artist and his friend.

A few minutes later, she turned and followed them. At the gates of Trevelyan House, the two men parted, and, with slow step and bent head, the artist again walked homewards.

And the woman followed also.

The roar of the traffic made continual murmur, the streets were full of hurrying cabs and people on business or pleasure intent, but the artist saw none of them. In the midst of the great crowd, he sounded the depths of solitude; in the microcosm where his fame had risen and would set, he walked as a man unknown. There was a light burning in the hall as he entered his house; it was a long, narrow entrance, with walls richly decorated and hung with engravings, in many of which his own works lived again in sombre outline. He entered the studio, where the light from hanging lamps diffused a gentle radiance, and he ascended the little flight of steps leading to the gallery and the smaller room above.

This he entered.

There was no light therein, save that which glimmered faintly upon the window-pane, a reflection from a neighbouring lamp. The artist threw open the window and looked out into the dark night. A wind had risen, and black clouds were hurrying across the murky heaven, veiling the pale, trembling stars. Below, the long lines of garden wall were dimly visible, and the swaying branches of the trees. Distance there was none; only the impenetrable veil of the thick atmosphere, beneath whose gloomy softness earth and sky were one.

And the wind whistled fiercely through the branches, making strange moans among the tall, dark trees, sinking ever and anon into a fitful slumber, from which it would again awake in fiercer tumult, like some agonised human soul.

The artist leaned his elbows on the window-sill and played with the thoughts that seemed to him in keeping with Nature's gloomy mood.

'It is like life,' he said to himself bitterly. 'A tumult and a fever, and a dreaming, restless sleep. A struggle with alien foes, with untoward circumstances, and what shall be the ending thereof?'

The light of the solitary lamp flickered wildly, the wind rushed over it and fled murmuring into the trees; it whistled into the chimneys also, and ruffled the feathers of the house sparrow in her nest.

The man standing by the window leaned his head upon his hands, and a cry went out from a soul in pain.

'I could bear it better without these glimpses of joy! One can toil on through a wilderness until the stones almost cease to cut one's feet, but when suddenly an oasis opens, and vanishes at one's approach, envy and discontent begin to murmur of what *might* have been. Why have those golden eyes crossed my path, like sunshine falling on dead leaves? Pshaw! what have I to do with sunshine?'

His hands clasped the window-sill tightly, his whole energies were enlisted in the intensity of the struggle that was before him.

'A false position,' he said aloud. 'Is it right to let it thus continue? Should I tell her—tell her everything? And yet, why trouble the serenity of her innocent life with such details? What would she care?'

In his disordered fancy it seemed to him that a voice spoke out of the darkness. 'We are very pleased to see you,' it said gently, and he tried to answer, but could not. Swiftly rose before him the spectre of his life, shadowing a cold, dark grave. Therein his youth lay buried.

Dumbly he stretched out his hands in the darkness; the wind leapt over them like a child at play. Bitterly the soul of him mourned for that lost youth lying crushed and mangled under the ashes of many years.   The man who is thus bereft bears an eternal sense of injury; he has lost the priceless good that honour, fame, or power can never restore to him; for it there is no substitute in this imperfect world.

The loneliness of his life made the deliberate decision more difficult; in a passion of self-pity, he told himself that such sacrifice as he contemplated must surely be made in vain; that it could be of no moment to Sybil whether his visits ceased abruptly or were continued at intervals.   What had a creature so full of sunshine to do with the successful, solitary man?   Why should he not be content to enjoy the occasional sweetness of those visits without tormenting himself with retrospect of foreboding?   Might not a fairer life, with richer developments, rise even now from the ashes of his scarred and blighted past?   The priceless boon of a woman's friendship was at stake—might he dare to win it?

The thought had many issues; he gazed with burning intensity into the dark veil of the night, he was thinking of Michal.

She, with her earnest, unfathomable eyes, seemed

to watch him, perhaps with pity; the clear soul
looked down upon his restlessness, surely com-
manding him to be true? Her voice was as the
voice of Conscience within him, but the hunger
for sympathy, for friendliness, conquered all other
instincts, and his weakness sheltered in compromise.

'I will go once again, as I said,' he murmured,
and he stepped back wearily into the little room.

A few minutes afterwards he walked into the
parlour where his evening meal awaited him, grave,
calm, and self-controlled. Many are the conflicts
that the world knows not of—fought out in silence,
covered with a smile—whose record, unchronicled
on earth, may dwell, perchance, in the eternal remembrance with all that ever has been or shall
be.

.   .   .   .

The hands of the calendar were travelling once
more over the sultry days of August; the sunshine
this afternoon was accompanied by a warm breeze
from the westward, which would probably, according to the Englishman's mournful experience, end
in rain. Michal Iliff was sitting deep in thought,
with her head thrown back upon the tiger-skin
which lay as usual over her chair. An open
volume of Horace had slipped from her lap on to
the ground, her mind was absorbed by personal
interests, and, for once, the solemn metre of that

living verse, which is the echo of ancient civilisation, failed to rivet her attention.

She was holding in her hand a letter which she had just opened and read, and her face wore its habitual look of earnest thought shadowed by some slight melancholy. The girls had returned from their visit a fortnight ago, and Sybil had embraced her daily routine at the studio with renewed energy after the wholesome rest. The month had passed very happily in the quiet seclusion of that country home, gladdened by the glimpse of familar faces in the life-giving air which they loved.

Gently, mindful of the artist's warning, had Michal watched over her friend, as Sybil, in the intervals of her joyous tranquillity, took up her painting once more. But she had not achieved very much, and the Poëtess noticed with the quick sympathy of love that the fits of inconsequent depression to which the artistic temperament is so subject, were of more frequent occurrence with her than heretofore.

One evening, in Sybil's absence, Michal and her kindly hostess sat talking over the details of their London life.

'Don't fall into the mistake of living too much out of the world, my dear,' the old lady had said gently. 'I don't mean that you yourself might be injured by solitude, but it would be hurtful to

Sybil. She needs change and the contact of new minds and ideas in her profession, and the studio life is merely a school. Remember, an artist belongs to Society, and must belong to it if he is to get on.'

Michal was a trifle pained.

'I don't think *solitude à deux* can ever be very trying to either of us,' she answered, 'and we have many resources in our lives, but I think I understand what you mean. You are speaking from the standpoint of worldly advantage.'

'Yes, my dear; from the standpoint of all practical people—not from that of a dreamer in the clouds. Forgive me, dear, if my frankness is brutal; an old woman is privileged, you know, and I love you both sincerely.'

Home truths, forcibly put, and Michal knew too well the sound sense and motherly kindness of the speaker to feel any resentment; but the words recurred to her now as she sat alone with that letter in her hand. It was a note from Lady Charlecote, asking them to dinner on the tenth.

'We really must see more of you before we migrate,' the letter ran, 'and we have arranged a charming little dinner-party on Tuesday, so put on your prettiest dresses and come. We shall be delighted to see you.'

The letter was addressed to Sybil, but the

Poetess, recognising the handwriting, had opened it. She read it over three or four times, and it made her thoughtful. She herself would so gladly have refused this invitation. She knew the type of the people she would be likely to meet, and did not desire them; the society represented by Lady Charlecote's *coterie* was an alien life to her; she was not in touch with their environment—it made her *genée*, impatient and rebellious, and it roused the bitter spirit of opposition which was soon kindled in her passionate and loyal breast.

For Michal, in the absorbing possession of her yet untried but dominant genius, shrank involuntarily from the worshipper of strange gods. She, like all others breathing the inspiration of the 'faculty divine,' took herself and her gift very seriously; and the earnest faith underlying her quest for truth, together with a humble, yet deep, belief in her mandate of utterance, gave rise also to a passionate scorn of mere self-seeking and sensuous lives.

Nevertheless, she began to feel herself impelled to make a sacrifice at the sacred shrine of her love.

Sybil, wandering like a bee among the varied flora of humanity, had a wonderful habit of extracting all the sweetness from the blossoms, ignoring only all faded and blemished growth. This power was the secret of her rare joyousness, her easy self-adaptation to changing modes of life.

'Where I see angels you see only ghosts,' she had once laughingly said to Michal; and the Poetess, with a strange feeling of humility, had taken the jest *au serieux*, realising its force.

She realised it now. Her loving thought, playing about the sweet memory of her darling, recalled Sybil's playfulness and innocent enjoyment of all recreation—recalled, too, the weary look that ever and anon would shadow the bright young face after a long day's work at the studio.

Was it not the privilege of love to minister in all things to the cares and pleasures of its object? And was the love in her of so poor a quality?

She folded the letter with a quick resolution. It was only right that Sybil should have all the enjoyment and change that might be attainable. The Poetess saw this now, and blamed herself with characteristic earnestness in that she had not recognised it earlier. She rose and began to occupy herself with some trifle of needlework. In these days she did not read so constantly, and a pen was seldom in her hand; she was living intensely in the present, and lacked the unfettered imagination and repose of soul that must prelude the sweet spontaneity of the poet.

Since their return from the country, the girls had

seen nothing of Leslie Vernon. Sybil often spoke of him, and Michal knew that she was looking forward with some degree of hope and interest to the visit thus delayed. The Poetess also joined freely in the frank discussion of their strange, pessimistic visitor; but there were reservations in her judgment which even Sybil could not probe. She was still brooding over her needlework when her friend came home; and then, upon Sybil's cheery entrance, she roused herself into a merrier mood.

'I have been trespassing on the privacy of your correspondence, *cara mia*,' she said lightly, tossing the letter across to Sybil over the inevitable cup of fragrant tea.

Sybil read the note through and looked up doubtfully.

'It would be—rather fun, I think,' she ventured.

'Of course it would,' said Michal promptly. 'You must write, dear, and accept, this evening.'

Sybil's eyes filled with wonder.

'Do *you* want to go, Poetess?'

'Certainly I do.'

The dark eyes smiled back happily at the questioning glance of Sybil, and the discussion was at an end.

On the night of the tenth, as Michal stood before her mirror, fastening a cluster of white *abutilons* in the folds of her black lace gown, a small voice at the door requested admission, and Sybil entered with a smile. The Poetess paused and took a silent survey of the graceful little figure in its soft black draperies and Honiton scarf. Some mauve and yellow orchids relieved the sombreness of the costume, which suited the wearer to perfection.

'Do I look nice, Poetess?' said Sybil, with the self-conscious timidity of one who anticipates a criticism or a compliment, and, for answer, Michal bent and kissed the auburn curls.

'Poetess,'—(this in a conciliatory voice)—'don't you think that you might wear some little ornament?'

Michal looked surprised.

'Are not the flowers enough?' she answered.

Sybil shook her head, and approached her friend with a winsome gesture of entreaty.

'I wish,' she said in a low voice, 'that you would wear—that necklace of—your mother's.'

She felt, rather than saw, the quick pain that leapt into the dark eyes, and she went on hurriedly.

'I have many jewels—these pearls I am wearing were my mother's; they are a remembrance of her, and they are beautiful. You have very few, and from an artistic point of view, my Poetess, there is something needed in your appearance to-night. The touch of delicate gold is just what you want. Why should you mind it, dear?'

Still silence.

'To please me,' said the little tempter, caressingly, and Michal yielded to the only power by which her own strong will was conquered. 'Shall I get it out, Poetess?'

'If you like, dear.'

And Michal stood in silent thought while the necklace was clasped about her neck by Sybil's eager fingers. It shone with a gleam of subdued lustre, and she turned away with a faint smile.

'So let it be, *carina*, as you wished it. That it is an improvement I will not deny.'

Sybil replaced the soft paper in the old tin box and closed it with a triumphant gesture. She was prouder of Michal's aristocratic charm than of her own fresh beauty, and she wished to augment Society's appreciation of her friend.

They drove up to the house in Eaton Square just as a brougham with the Trevelyan liveries was moving away in an opposite direction.

'Who is that girl in black with the *abutilons?*' said a dowager, levelling an eye-glass at Michal, when the girls had entered the room and exchanged the usual greetings.

Lady Charlecote replied, with alacrity,—

'That is Miss Iliff, the ward of my poor cousin Frank (Colonel Murray, you know), who was in India so long—died only last year, poor fellow.'

'Ah! not bad-looking,' was the dispassionate comment of the dowager, as she turned her small head, with its dainty *coiffure*, in another direction.

'I call her very distinguished-looking,' said the hostess, instantly on her defence, and she moved away to do honour to the young Bulgarian ambassador, who had just appeared upon the threshold.

The richly-decorated room presented a charming effect of colour under the soft light of many candles; the guests were only twelve in number, and Lady Charlecote shrewdly congratulated herself upon the remarkably well-assorted gathering.

Sir John's habitual expression of boredom relaxed somewhat at a dinner-party where at least there was always the anticipation of a convivial after-dinner chat, and his face lightened up with positive pleasure upon beholding the auburn head of Sybil. He devoted himself to her until the dinner-hour was announced, when their interests became suddenly diverse—he being under the necessity of offering his arm to the dowager with the eye-glass, while Sybil was placed under the escort of an energetic young barrister-at-law. She found the situation pleasant and entertaining; the young member of the learned profession was gifted with a vast eloquence and encumbered with some superfluous wit. He found Sybil a listener after his own heart—sympathetic and amused. She glanced from time to time round the table at the various guests, and her glance rested most frequently upon the lovely, diamond-crowned head of Lady Trevelyan.

'And that is the Earl,' she thought, with a faint sense of curiosity, as she looked across at the grave man who was sitting next to Michal. 'He looks as proud as his wife, and as unbending. What can Leslie Vernon find in common with him, I wonder?'

Her glance met that of Michal, and she smiled happily.

The Poetess was engaged in an earnest conversation with the ardent young Socialist, who had fallen to her share. He was the second son of a Tory baron, and had adopted views which threatened to sow discord among the members of his house. But Michal was interested; it was, at least, she thought, a satisfaction to have found someone brimming over with enthusiasm, and there was certainly no tameness about this stranger. He waved the red flag of Socialism boldly in the face of the horrified dowager and of the patient host, and finally he devoted himself and his arguments to Michal.

An interesting combat ensued. The young man abandoned his whitebait in his eagerness to defend the dogma of equality, the logical soundness of its

theoretical basis as granted by Mill, the justice of
its practical application in a world where inequality
had run riot.

Michal opposed him on the ground of biological
science.

'You would place an iron bar in the road of progress,' she answered. 'Does not inequality exist
in the earliest stages of all existence, down to the
living germ of protoplasm in the reproductive cell?
You would annihilate, with "one fell swoop," all
theories of evolution—all evidence of the struggle
for life which is the outcome of individual in-
equalities. What reason have we for supposing
that such will ever cease to exist? And in practice,
would your theory, do you think, found an
Utopia?'

'Yes,' he replied boldly. 'A world where all
men were equal would allow less scope for vice:
envy and the perpetual prejudices of caste would
not lead to the crimes which are every day committed under our system.'

'But you lose the virtues also,' she objected.
'They must be sacrificed.'

'Which of them?'

She smiled faintly.

'What would become of pity, mercy, benevol-
ence in your flat world of sameness? You may
perhaps consider all these virtues as forms of self-

indulgence, but yet they count for something in the scheme of life.'

He shifted his ground impatiently.

'That is mere sentiment,' he answered. 'We wish to base our principles on purely utilitarian grounds; we believe that the system is the best attainable under the circumstances; we do not say that it is ideally perfect, neither do we assume that every man is mentally equipped up to precisely the same standard. So there would still be room for your virtues to have fair play, and every man ought to have a fair chance in life's battle.'

'Yes, she assented eagerly, 'and every woman too. But to that end surely all progress is tending. The centuries will find us gradually less handicapped; at least, that is my ardent hope and belief.'

'America is the only nation that has shown an independent example so far,' said the young man, with decision.

Michal's neighbour turned round slowly and surveyed both combatants with a slight smile. He had overheard some of the discussion, being attracted by the musical voice of Michal.

'You seem to adhere to the Aristotelian precept, that "Virtue lies in the mean,"' he said quietly.

She was taken aback and did not immediately reply.

'It is all very well for you, my lord, to be cynical,' said the young man grimly. 'You are, at present, on the winning side.'

There was a pause.

The grave glance of the Earl travelled slowly from the somewhat averted face of the Poetess, and rested upon her necklace with a scrutiny by no means characteristic of the well-bred Peer. He did not speak, and Sybil, looking across at him, saw the face of a man who is suddenly confronted by a long-banished and forgotten memory. The conversation buzzed round him, and the butler came to him with a choice of wines, but he heard nothing. The time had changed suddenly for him: he was again in his youth.

'Such a strange thing happened to us on Saturday,' said the lady on his right. 'We took a box at the Lyceum, and—'

He started with a vague sense of alarm, and turned with a smile and an apology.

And Sybil saw and wondered.

'I brought out this portfolio of old prints, Sybil, knowing that you, as an artist, would appreciate them,' said Lady Charlecote, after the guests had all reassembled in the drawing-room. 'Some of them are very old and valuable, and I daresay you would like to look them over.'

Sybil blushed at this public recognition, but moved with alacrity towards the little table on which the portfolio lay.

Michal and a few others joined her in the inspection of the prints, some of which were, as the hostess had said, of considerable age and value, and Sybil was not the only one who appreciated the treat.

'There are some modern engravings amongst them,' observed the Poetess, as she took up a print bearing the date ef eighteen hundred and seventy. 'Surely I know this picture; I mean, I have seen it engraved before.'

'It is one of Mr Vernon's,' said Sybil promptly, glancing over her friend's shoulder. '"The Reprieve"—it was considered one of his best works, I believe.'

'And justly so,' said a quiet voice, at whose utterance Sybil turned involuntarily. 'For my own part, I am proud to have become the possessor.'

It was Lord .Trevelyan who spoke, and he was looking, at the same time, with a little smile at Sybil. Somewhere he had seen her face before; what memory did it recall to him?

'*You*—you know Mr Vernon?' she hazarded in a lame fashion, half shy and half eager; and then he remembered, and smiled again with the peculiar quiet courtesy which was his habitual attitude towards women.

'We speak of a mutual acquaintance, I think,' he said pleasantly. 'Are you not Miss Murray?'

The deep blush which accompanied her answer surprised and amused him. Had the cynical Vernon developed an *entêtement* with this auburn-haired maiden, he wondered. The thought amused him vastly, and he remembered the German poetry upon the rough sketch. His tact, however, forbade him to pursue the subject, and the conversation took a more technical colouring over the discussion of the prints. Suddenly he raised his eyes and beheld the Poetess, who had become unaccountably silent. Their eyes met for an instant, and Lord Trevelyan turned away.

Michal was troubled, and her restlessness betrayed itself in the black depths of her eyes. She, too, had noticed Sybil's blush, and had resented it with an unreasonable sense of anger against the Earl; something in his calm, self-possessed manner jarred painfully upon her nerves; she tried to conquer her aversion, but could not.

During their drive home that night, Michal was very silent. Sybil, with her tumbled hair resting against her friend's shoulder, kept up an incessant chatter all by herself, satisfied with an occasional reply.

'You are not tired, darling?' said the Poetess, as they threw off their wraps in the sitting-room.

'Tired!' The little fresh face laughed back at her in scorn. 'I have enjoyed the evening, Poetess —it was great fun, and I liked every one, except, perhaps, that grim old Earl. I watched him at dinner-time, Poetess, and I know that he saw a ghost.'

'What! in his right-hand neighbour?'

'No.' Sybil shook her head impressively. 'He was looking at you, and then, suddenly, he thought of something and became grey. I was quite sorry for him.'

'A guilty conscience, perhaps,' said her friend, with a faint smile.

'Perhaps.' Sybil became thoughtful. 'I can't think how he guessed my name, or rather knew it,' she observed presently.

Michal made a movement of slight impatience.

'If Mr Vernon has spoken of you, which is more than probable, I think the mystery is soon solved,' she answered, 'and it is too late for meditation now ; so, my little friend, good-night.'

'Why is it more than probable, I wonder?' thought Sybil perversely, as she went upstairs. 'And if he did talk about me, why doesn't he come again ? But the mystery is not solved yet, be-cause—'

She gave her head a little shake, such medita-tions savoured of foolishness ; she would think of to-morrow's work at the studio, and not of Leslie Vernon.

CHAPTER XI.

'Eyelids stored with arrows ready drawn.'

ON the following day Mr Stanton, the butler at Trevelyan House, heard the great door-bell clang noisily as he was crossing the hall. It was dusk, and he was just about to make some slow and stately preparations for the dinner-hour; the sound disturbed his meditations upon the peculiar merits of Amontillado and Chablis, and he walked leisurely to answer the summons.

'Is milord at home?' said a deep voice, with a foreign pronunciation.

Mr Stanton peered curiously at the tall figure of a woman enveloped in a cloak and shawl.

'Lord Trevelyan is not at home,' he replied stiffly, and considered the interview at an end.

But the woman advanced with a swiftness to which his measured steps were unaccustomed, and thrust her foot in the doorway.

'I come in,' she said, 'and wait for him.'

Mr Stanton looked down at the large, rough boot in dismay.

'You must go round to the back entrance,' he answered. 'This door is only for his lordship's friends, and you cannot come in and wait. You had better call again—at the back entrance.'

And the great door moved upon its hinges with such evident intent of banishment that the woman withdrew her foot and shrank away, flinging back, as she did so, an angry reply,—

'*Che?* Milord's friends! Not his enemies— ha! ha!'

And Mr Stanton, carefully replacing the latch of the front door, heard the sound of harsh, muttering laughter, and he shook his head over the increasing audacity of the beggar tribe. It grieved his self-respect that he should have demeaned himself so as to answer such a summons. He spoke of the incident to no one on that account.

And the woman went slowly down the steps and paused by the great gates of Trevelyan House to look back upon the smoke-grimed, substantial dwelling. She did not speak, but there was that in her burning eyes that rendered speech superfluous; the earnest soul gleamed forth from them, savage, tumultuous, like a tiger escaped from its chain. She gathered her shawl more closely about her and set off at a quick pace northward, never pausing until she had reached the door of Leslie Vernon's house in St John's Wood, where, as before, she gave a noisy appeal for entrance.

'Is Signor—Mr Vernon at home?' she said slowly, the English titles being, as it appeared, somewhat tormenting to her tongue.

'Yes, do you wish to see him?' said the house-maid.

A strange smile crossed the woman's face as she entered the hall without further ceremony. This reception was different, she thought.

After the lapse of a few minutes she was ushered into the studio, where the artist sat reading under one of the hanging red lamps. He rose and threw aside his cigar, and looked inquiringly at the visitor.

'Will you sit down?' he said gravely, 'and tell me your business?'

He had a peculiarly quiet and even courteous manner with his inferiors, which won him confidence and liking. The woman's dark eyes softened a little as she took the proffered seat and let her shawl slip gently from her shoulders, revealing the folded muslin and picturesque detail of her attire.

'*Parlate Italiano?*' she said abruptly.

'Not much, I am afraid,' said Leslie Vernon. 'I fear I must ask you to explain your errand in English.'

'*Ebbene*—I come to ask—you paint pictures—
do you desire model?'

He smiled.

'I am very glad sometimes of a good model,' he
said pleasantly. 'Have you had any experience?'

'I sat in studio at Signor Raffini and Signor
Ashley, and some more.'

He rose and lighted the lamp which swung
above the head of his visitor, and she looked up
and met the full light boldly.

'*Io era bella ma—*' she began, and corrected
herself suddenly—'I am no more beautiful, but
they say I make a good model.'

She stood upright, folded her arms and looked
at him. But the artist gave hardly more than a
passing glance at the supple beauty of her tall
figure, nor even at the rugged grandeur of the
countenance shaded by its mass of loosely-braided
hair, he saw only the fierce dark eyes that gleamed
at him from their sunken sockets, and they reminded him of a wild cat that he had once seen
maddened by captivity. Awful eyes they were—
he thought of them with a shudder, and wished
that his memory were, for the moment, less strong.

Then he said aloud with hesitation,—

'I am not working at any important picture just
now, but I should like to make a study of you—a
portrait.'

Will next Thursday morning suit you, at ten o'clock?'

She smiled—a strange, triumphant smile, and it seemed to him like the exultation of a fiend. He wondered vaguely whether a nearer acquaintance with his model would prove her to be mad or merely vicious; the experiment might be interesting, after all. He rose and dismissed her courteously.

'You speak English very well,' he said, as an after-thought. 'Have you been long in England?'

'Twelve months; but I have learnt long time in Italy. Good-night, signor.'

'Good-night,' said Leslie Vernon, returning to his cigar and his book.

CHAPTER XII.

'The dry light of criticism.'

THE following Saturday afternoon was wet and gloomy; he worked in a desultory way for a couple of hours, and then threw down his brush.

'No light,' he said impatiently.

A restlessness had come upon him, and a longing which he could no longer withstand, and which was growing daily stronger, overcame his prudence and resolves—he took up his old felt hat and went out.

Michal, glancing out of the window as she crossed the room, beheld the familiar figure advancing, and said quietly,—

'Mr Vernon is in search of recreation on this gloomy day, *carina*. I think he is coming here.'

There was an instant upheaval at the other end of the room as Sybil sprang up from her easel, tore off her apron, and flung her canvas aside.

'Do come, Poetess, and help me to clear away these things, or else shut the doors, or do some-

H

thing. I would not have him see this abominable study for the world; and oh! Poetess, be quick—I am so afraid of him and of his criticism.'

But Michal did not share the alarm, and when Leslie Vernon entered the room a few moments later, Sybil was discoverable in a somewhat forced attitude of repose, while her friend was standing near the denuded easel, holding a mahlstick in her hand.

The interchange of greetings under these circumstances was a trifle less free than of old, and the artist's quick intelligence grasped the situation.

'Don't let me disturb you,' he said pleasantly, 'though I expect you, like myself, find the light to-day atrocious.'

Sybil's blush rose vividly.

'How did you guess I was painting?' she said.

'Partly from your own confession. You wore the inevitable conscious look that is the brand of the guilty who sins at rare intervals and in broad daylight. Miss Iliff, moreover, was brandishing the mahlstick in a peculiarly defiant manner; and you will pardon my drawing your attention to a patch of white upon your sleeve.'

She did pardon it, and an air of better understanding arose.

'It is one of the penalities of my position,' said the artist, 'that lesser lights have a tendency to eclipse themselves instantaneously upon my entrance—it is nevertheless one of my few privileges to try and assist such modest little lights to burn more steadily.'

He bent his gaze kindly upon Sybil.

'I see one good result of your holiday in your face; what about the other result? Did you work much, or did you follow my sage advice and rest entirely?'

'A medium course,' laughed Sybil. 'I did only a few sketches, and most of them studies, merely.'

'That was good; and are they for ever entombed in some deep sepulchre, wherein the eye of man may not penetrate?'

'The eye of the critic,' said Michal, 'is sometimes as much to be feared as to be courted—at least, that is Sybil's view.'

'Yes; she is a very modest little light,' he answered gently; and the Poetess caught the softer gleam in his eyes, and said no more.

She sat very silently while he looked at the sketches which, after some further hesitation, Sybil had produced. It was with a strange mixture of satisfaction and uneasiness that she listened to the accurate, unsparing criticism, and noted its effect upon her friend. 'She would not have borne that from anyone else,' and 'he would not take the trouble for anyone but her,' were the thoughts that arose in her mind and kept her silent. Not that she was needed to swell the conversation; the artist and Sybil were too thoroughly engrossed in their subject to need the prompting of a third.

Leslie Vernon was roused for once into the full exercise of his artistic faculty—he was at his best. The trained accuracy of the artist, the bald frankness of a cynic, and a touch of latent poetry which almost imperceptibly softened the polished angles of his thoughts and their expression—all combined to heighten the charm of his personality.

The Poetess felt this strongly, and Sybil listened with shining eyes.

'This is the piece I like best, after all,' he said, taking up, for the fourth time, a small landscape in oil. 'It has the best treatment, though it is too ambitious. There is enough material in it for three pictures, and you have tried to condense it all into one. The fault of the tyro—in art, in literature, in life—is ever the same; he overcrowds his canvas, so that the harmony of the whole is lost—it ceases to have a central idea: it is no longer a unity, but a kaleidoscope. A picture, a book, a poem, should have a nucleus, a central thought, around which the accessories are judiciously blended, all conducing to the same end— not too prominent, not too numerous, but just sufficient to give force to the interpretation. You have painted this for the sake of painting, not for the sake of interpreting what you saw.'

'I suppose,' said Sybil timidly, 'that everything in Art is symbolic—that is what you mean by interpretation?'

'Just so,' he answered; 'and therein lies the essence of true Art. What is the sky worth to you if it does not suggest infinity? What the mighty girth of an oak, if not power? What the gentle, parallel lines of pasture land, if not repose? Do we love the face of a child but for its fresh innocence? and when we paint the head of a dog, we do not immortalise the curves and the colouring, but the expression of unwavering and absolute fidelity. A rustic once said to Rousseau, "Why do you make that tree when it is already made?" He could not understand that the artist was not painting the tree as he understood it—he was endeavouring to clothe the idea which the tree had suggested to him, and would suggest to the thoughtful student of Nature.'

There was a pause. Sybil, following out the train of thought thus awakened, had no words to spare.

The artist looked again at the sketch, and continued—

'Another stumbling-block to you is shadow. The shadows here are not all true. This one,

thrown by the fence upon the ground, is out of
harmony with the contiguous tones.   Here, again,
you have painted too much and learnt too little.
You have not realised the wonder and the beauty
of shadow in the world.'

'That is a long thought,' said Michal.   'Fancy a
world from which shadow is withdrawn !   You cannot.   Light goes also, and with it all colour, till we
are merged in a chaos of darkness.'

'Yes : everything has its so-called complement,'
said the artist, ' and its own relative value.   Rightly
to determine such values is perhaps the secret of
genius joined to a simplicity of expression, which
is the highest skill.'

'That simplicity is born, not made,' said Sybil.

'Spontaneity is a gift—an attribute of the individual,' he answered.   'But it may be cultivated
or spoilt.   If you study method all your life, and
method only, you will have a skilfulness of touch,
but not spontaneity, and no sacred fire.   Impres-
sionism, rightly understood, is a spontaneous expression of touch—a sixth sense, someone has
called it.'

Sybil took the sketches from him and laid them
aside.

'I cannot look at them any more,' she said
appealingly.

In her eyes shone a pathetic expression of

humilty and wistfulness. She had measured her feeble stature against the lofty standard of his trained intelligence, and had fallen back bruised and desponding.

He saw it, and his heart went out to her in her weakness. The desire to help is one of the strongest impulses of a strong soul. He who knows, burns to impart his knowledge; he who loves, to benefit the object beloved; he who has a message, to proclaim it to all mankind. Altruism, after all, is not so rare a thing among the baser growths of humanity.

'Little girl,' said the artist, gently, 'you must not be discouraged. You would not wish us to lower the standard of our highest endeavour because you cannot reach it at one bound? Mind, I do not tell you that you will never reach it. I tell you to wait, and to learn, and to study the noblest patterns. I have spoken the truth to you because I never think it worth my while to do otherwise. I hold it a despicable thing to lie to a woman through a false sense of politeness.

The Poetess looked up with sparkling eyes.

'Well spoken,' she said, warmly. 'We should neither of us value your criticism if we detected a false ring. As it is—'

'As it is,' echoed Sybil, with a cheery nod, 'we value it immensely, and I am beginning to recover myself after a few shocks, and feel much better.'

But despite this assurance, the artist was not completely satisfied.

'Do you often go to the National Gallery?' he said.

'Only on Saturday afternoons — occasionally. My other days, as you know, are filled up.'

'Could you both spare me an hour next Saturday, and allow me to try to be your guide in one or two instances? There are some gems of Turner, Constable and Claude that may either have escaped your notice, or, if you do know them, may be almost too familiar to be striking to you.'

The joy that leapt into the golden eyes made his heart beat faster.

'It would be lovely!' she answered, with a little sigh of content.

He looked at Michal, and met her grave smile. She also looked glad and grateful, he thought with a sense of satisfaction.

Tea was brought, and they talked gaily over the events, public and personal, of the last month. Sybil, in a merry mood, chattered incessantly of the studio, of Lady Charlecote's dinner party, and of their slight acquaintance with Lord Treveylan.

But on this last topic the artist was somewhat taciturn.

'Do you think they love one another?' asked Sybil suddenly.

Leslie Vernon looked up in amaze.

'What! Trevelyan and his wife? I should be very much surprised if they had ever thought of such a thing. They are married, that's all.'

The sweet eyes grew a trifle sad.

The Poetess smiled, and answered lightly,—

'You mean that he has gained a beautiful woman to entertain his "*clientèle*," and she has gained the not uncommon bargain of a "strong dose of animalism," as Schopenhauer would say.'

The grim irony of this remark, he felt, was deeply rooted in the girl's passionate soul.

He answered only by a slight gesture of indifference, and began to speak of other things. During his walk home that night a strange exultation seized him; a new-born joyousness—irrational, unshadowed—filled his heart with its vivifying power. He looked round, and lo! the great world stretched out before him as a paradise, bright with the chorus of songs innumerable, blossoming with all pure and lovely things. He did not pause to wonder why it was so, he only knew that it blossomed, that it sang. The grim world of reality, with its full tide of woe, swept back from his feet as he trod the sunlit path of imagination. Before his world-stained eyes the gates of love were opening wide their portals. He wandered therein content.

Those are rare exalted moments when the soul, rising by the power of Love beyond the personal selfishness of the Ego, and holding fast to its pure ideal, as it were to the hem of God's skirt, breathes the very essence of the Divine. Such moments leave their mark upon the record of individual life. They remain, and will remain, when other things have faded into the ashes of oblivion.

CHAPTER XIII.

'No woman art thou, but a lioness or monster of the sea.'
Stories from the Greek Tragedians.

THE days that followed brought a revival of youth
and energy into the life of Leslie Vernon. The
Saturday afternoon at the National Gallery was
followed by many other Saturdays spent after the
same fashion, and these proved to be red-letter
days in the solitary life of the artist. A new
enthusiasm possessed him, and as he and the two
girls wandered from one fragment to another of
the well-known collection, he discovered beauties
that he had never seen before; the happiness that
filled his soul overflowed in its exuberance; it
made him eloquent, impassioned, strong.

The girls were not uninfluenced by the change in
him. Sybil's enthusiasm leapt forth to meet his
own. She lived on those Saturday afternoons in
an ideal world peopled by her own imaginations;
the pictures were no longer inanimate echoes of a
great master, they were living friends. The Re-

naissance was no longer a far-off historical epoch;
she inhaled the very essence of its ambition and its
art.

Michal also felt the spell of these influences, and
the old perplexity that had so often made her restless was almost charmed away. Now and then she
would glance at the impassioned face of the artist
with the lovelight shining through his eyes, and
then she would grow grave again, oppressed by a
weight of uncertainty. But Sybil's supreme and
unshadowed happiness was infectious after its kind;
the pure joy that radiated from her sunny nature
had a never-failing source, and, in these days she
shone perpetually. Passers-by, meeting the glance
of the sweet, candid eyes, would turn and look again
at her—Michal noticed it with a thrill of loving
pride.

Nevertheless, at times, she would ponder a little
uneasily. '*En devenant Artiste, elle n'a pas cessée
d'être femme,*' she said to herself, with the shrewd
philosophy of an onlooker who sympathises intensely with the developments and weaknesses
which he himself has never known.

The autumn crept on apace; the *beau monde*
began to break up, as many of its members
migrated to the country houses in view of pheasant
and grouse shooting. The Trevelyans were among
the number. Sir John and Lady Charlecote

lingered a little longer, but in October they also vanished, and the house in Eaton Square was a mournful monument of desolation.

On one of the Saturdays devoted to the National Gallery, Leslie Vernon made an unusual confession.

'I want a subject for a picture,' he said.

The girls looked surprised.

'Is your imagination so much at fault?' said Sybil saucily. 'It would be wiser not to confess it. Your reputation might suffer.'

'Reputation be hanged!' he retorted grimly. 'I will tell you what I mean. I have been painting a portrait from a model unique in my experience—a fierce-eyed, desperate-looking Italian woman—not young, but altogether the most striking person that I have ever tried to depict. A great wish has seized me to make her the subject of a more ambitious venture.'

'We had a woman such as you describe,' said Sybil, 'at the studio some months ago. I shall never forget her face; it used to haunt me—I never could shake off the impression that I had seen it somewhere before, though, of course, that was unfounded.'

'Did you succeed in the likeness?' asked Leslie Vernon.

'Not at all, to my idea. There seemed to be

something in her eyes that defied portraiture—at least—' she corrected herself smiling, 'it defied my attempts and those of the students around me. In your hands it would be different. Do carry out that idea—I am sure it would repay you.'

'I cannot at present identify her,' he answered thoughtfully, 'either with an abstract idea or with any heroine of myth or history. The Grecian anthropomorphism is full of suggestiveness, but at present I have found nothing to suit my mood and my model.'

'The story of Hagar,' said the Poetess, 'always seems to me to lend itself readily to artistic interpretation. The Hebrew outcast might have looked out on the wilderness with eyes such as Sybil has described.'

'True, but it is a subject that has already been attacked,' he answered. 'I should like to cut out a fresh path for my female ruffian. She interests me vastly.'

'Have you heard anything about her former life?' asked Sybil. 'We never could extract a syllable from her.'

'She is not so reticent now as at first,' replied Leslie Vernon. 'Indeed, she betrays a somewhat vivid curiosity at times in the sketches and portraits that I may have lying about the room. My sketch in charcoal of Lord Trevelyan, for instance, and something in her eyes that defied portraiture—at least—' she corrected herself smiling, 'it defied my attempts and those of the students around me. In your hands it would be different. Do carry out that idea—I am sure it would repay you.'

'I cannot at present identify her,' he answered thoughtfully, 'either with an abstract idea or with any heroine of myth or history. The Grecian anthropomorphism is full of suggestiveness, but at present I have found nothing to suit my mood and my model.'

'The story of Hagar,' said the Poetess, 'always seems to me to lend itself readily to artistic interpretation. The Hebrew outcast might have looked out on the wilderness with eyes such as Sybil has described.'

'True, but it is a subject that has already been attacked,' he answered. 'I should like to cut out a fresh path for my female ruffian. She interests me vastly.'

'Have you heard anything about her former life?' asked Sybil. 'We never could extract a syllable from her.'

'She is not so reticent now as at first,' replied Leslie Vernon. 'Indeed, she betrays a somewhat vivid curiosity at times in the sketches and portraits that I may have lying about the room. My sketch in charcoal of Lord Trevelyan, for instance, and

from it a volume of Euripides and read hastily
here and there a fragment of the well-known tale.
From the far-off past, from the land of the gods,
from the golden clouds of Olympus—it sprang
again into life and reality. The story of the
Golden Fleece was no longer myth but an actual
occurrence; the cramped type faded as he read,
and the page glowed with the faces of its gods and
heroines.

There was Jason, full of ambition as of courage,
setting forth to gain the Fleece of Gold. Medea,
the enchantress, was with him, her woman's love
and her witch's art were the strength of his right
hand. But the heart of Jason was unfaithful, and
wandered from his love.

He raised his eyes to the picture.

'Vengeance! The vengeance of Medea!' shrieked
the portrait.

He threw down the volume and stood again
before the easel in deep and active thought. There
was no need to read any further; the eyes told
him all that the tragedy contained, and much more.
Was not this woman capable of all that Medea
had accomplished by her magic and her cunning?
He felt sure that she was. An English paraphrase
of the old-world story was also in his possession;
he went in search of it and read again :—

'Very grievous is the deed that I must do when

this shall have been accomplished. For after this I must slay my children. Nor shall any man deliver them out of my hand. Thus will I destroy the whole house of Jason, and so depart from the land.'

He closed the book, and sat down; the problem was solved for him, and he sat playing with the new thought for hours.

Despite the fogs, to which they had hitherto been unaccustomed, the two girls found much gladness in their London life at this time.

Sybil, working steadily and happily, was conscious of a growing power; and her artistic faculty received its highest impressions from the generous hand of Leslie Vernon. She was radiantly happy; just sufficiently absorbed in her work as to derive much joy from its exercise, yet, withal, possessing a mind still open to the sweet influences of their home. Michal's love had never met with more instant and demonstrative sympathy, and the varied resources of their cheery life had never been by either more thoroughly enjoyed.

Their visitors, now that Lady Charlecote had departed for the season, were very few; St James's Hall and the Museum were their principal recreation grounds, and the frequent Saturday afternoons at the National and other Galleries kept up, in a manner profitable alike and pleasant, their acquaintance with Leslie Vernon.

I

It could hardly be called friendship, in spite of this constant intercourse; his manner, though unvaryingly pleasant and free, had, nevertheless, a certain limitation which Michal was not slow to recognise. The opinion which she gradually formed of him was not unfavourable; she thought him honourable, straightforward and true; but, beyond this, she could be sure of nothing.

One day, early in December, he came to them and said,—

'Will you come and look round my studio?'

Sybil's eyes sparkled.

'That is very kind of you,' she answered. 'We should like to come very much.'

There was a gleam of subdued triumph in his eyes as, a few days later, he met them at the door of his house, and ushered them into the studio.

Sybil was very silent, and a little shy: it was the mood in which he loved her best. With a stern self-repression he addressed himself principally to Michal, whilst producing the sketches and relics which he knew would interest them both.

'By-the-bye, what about that subject?' asked the Poetess, a sudden light of recollection awakening in her dreamy eyes. 'Have you begun your picture?'

'I have,' he answered slowly, with his eyes bent on the ground.

Then he went to his easel, and brought a large canvas into view.

'It is your turn to criticise,' he said simply.

Then he fell back a little, and stole a glance at Sybil's face in profile. He knew exactly what he should see there. He saw it, and it gave him a feeling of exultation that made his heart feel young.

Wonder, delight, and awe spoke in the changing lines of her delicate features. She grew silent and absorbed.

The picture glowed with an intensity of meaning which seemed to pervade the room, It was an impersonation of tragedy in the Aristotelian sense of the word ; the myth, once but a fragment of an old-world idealism, had now received an interpretation that augmented its power and pathos, making its reality more real. The desperate anguish of a revengeful, undisciplined soul leapt from the canvas as an embodied idea to which the clothing, however exquisite, of delicate technique and detail, was subservient.

The majestic figure of the enchantress was clad in the simple garments of the Hellenic age ; a white chiton, fastening on the shoulder with clasps, and drawn in at the waist under a golden girdle, fell in long, straight folds to her feet ; serpents of gold, encircling the upper arm, were her only ornaments, and a purple himation, slipping from her shoulders, swept the ground where the bodies of her murdered children lay.

The deed of vengeance was accomplished—in the background the chariot, with its winged dragons, was just appearing to further her escape.

And the woman herself, transformed by her overwhelming passion, stood remorseless and defiant in this terrible moment of her revenge. No longer was she the 'lady of sorrows,' lamenting the lost love of a faithless spouse, but a true barbarian whose passions, untempered by the graces of Hellenic civilisation, held her completely in their sway.

Nevertheless, upon the fierce, defiant countenance traces of beauty yet remained, and a certain dignity also, such as became a daughter of the Sun god's race, 'sprung of a noble sire.'

So intent was the artist in his survey of Sybil, that he had no eyes to spare for the Poetess. He did not see the look of pain, almost of terror, that had flashed into her eyes ; he did not see that she was trembling with a rush of emotion which she could not interpret, and which was foreign to her self-control.

She was the first to speak, and she turned towards him with hands outstretched a little, as though to push away some objectionable thing.

'You have summoned a fiend from Dante's Inferno,' she said, in a low voice, 'clothed in a woman's form.'

'Ah! So Jason thought,' said the artist, smiling. '"No woman art thou, but a lioness or a monster of the sea!"'

'What! Is it Medea, then?' said Sybil, turning her admiring eyes from the canvas.

'Yes,' he answered. 'The vengeance of Medea.'

CHAPTER XIV.

Canst thou not minister to a mind diseased,
Pluck from the memory a rooted sorrow,
Raze out the written troubles of the brain,
And, with some sweet oblivious antidote,
Cleanse the stuff'd bosom of that perilous stuff
Which weighs upon the heart?—*Macbeth.*

'IT is wonderful!' repeated Sybil, as she gazed with a sense of fascination and awe. 'It is the woman herself, with something added—something more.'

And, speaking, she turned and looked at Michal. Suddenly, a thought had flashed upon her consciousness, which drove the speech from her lips. For it was no longer the calm, pure face of the Poetess which she saw there; it was the likeness of Medea. She knew now why that woman's face had haunted her—why it had seemed familiar. It was not the features, not the expression in which the likeness lingered, but a look only—an occasional look that she knew. In that same moment her glance encountered that of the artist, and the thought passed back from his eyes.

With a sense of pained bewilderment, Sybil slipped her hand into that of Michal. ' The firm grasp of the Poetess caused an instant reaction, and she laughed back reassuringly into the inquiring eyes of her friend.

'You are sad also, Poetess,' she said. 'Methinks, if Mr Vernon's picture is going to have the same effect upon every one, the Academy next year will be a doleful exhibition. Will you not paint something fresh and pretty, Mr Vernon, by way of contrast?'

'Yes, if you will sit for me,' he answered laughingly, 'and make the most perfect contrast that I know.'

The blush, so easily provoked, rose immediately, their eyes met in a long, full glance, and Sybil turned suddenly away.

After that, their talk grew freer and more untrammelled, and they spent a pleasant hour among the treasures which the artist had accumulated, and which he so seldom displayed.

It was growing dusk when the girls left him; he returned slowly to the studio and mechanically lighted one of the hanging lamps.

'Will you have tea, sir?' said the servant, looking in at the door.

'No,' he answered wearily. 'I wish for nothing, thank you.'

And she closed the door upon him quietly.

He went up to the easel and stood there for a long time, looking straight in front of him in troubled, anxious thought. But it was not of the picture that he was thinking—not of his engrossing work.

The inspiration, the artistic enthusiasm which had absorbed his faculties so earnestly during these latter months, now fell away from him like a veil.

From his tired eyes the naked, suffering soul of a man looked forth upon its solitary world. That one glance from Sybil's eyes had re-awakened in his sensitive nature the old perplexity, the old doubt. It arose again with its scorching breath of despair and foreboding; it made him feel faint and dizzy with an actual physical pain.

He dropped into a chair with a low moan, and covered his face with his hands. The problem of his life stood facing him, he could not swerve or escape; and so, with the desperate energy of a man who stakes for life or death, he laid hold of it and struggled fiercely. He was not made of the stuff that builds up saints and heroes, neither could he rejoice in self-sacrifice for its own sake, with a smile for the fire and the sword; he was only a weak and sensitive man, embittered by a full cup of disappointment, soured by an irremediable wrong. Yet he was true to the light that was in him, with

a strong sense of honour that remained to the end;
he was also humble in his own self-estimate. Was
it possible, was it even probable, he asked himself,
that the love of so sunny a creature as Sybil could
ever have been attracted towards himself? In
other circumstances the thought would have intoxicated him with its passing sweetness; as it was, it
stabbed him with unendurable pain. He had never
thought of it before so strongly; but that look in
her sweet eyes had burned into his memory, and
haunted him still with undreamt-of possibilities
of sorrow and wrong. Was he acting rightly,
honestly? He knew that he was not.

The night crept up around him and veiled the
dim branches of the trees. The objects in the room
shewed faintly under the soft red light of the lamp,
and only the great canvas stood out clearly from
the background. The fierce eyes of the enchantress seemed to be watching him; he sat in unbroken silence, with his head bowed upon his hands.
When he rose, there was a look in his countenance
which bore witness to the weight of added years.
For age does not move with the calendar, neither
can it be reckoned by days; it is the sum of our
emotions, of our knowledge, and of our pain.

The next day the artist spent in desultory occupation until twilight began to fall. Then he rose,
took his hat, and went out. Some strange emotion

made him pause on the threshold and look round the quiet studio before leaving. It seemed to his distorted fancy that the inanimate things must be in harmony with his mood. He looked at them as though taking a long farewell; he was going to face a crisis of his life; how would it all look when he returned?

He closed the door abruptly and went forth. His pre-occupation was so strong that, on arriving at the house in Maida Vale, he forgot the preliminary forms of greeting, and entered the hall without a word. But the girl knew him, and ushered him, without protest, into the presence of Michal. The Poetess was sitting by the fireside, a book of manuscript upon her knee. She rose to greet him with the easy dignity characteristic of her, and bade him sit down.

Then, for the first time, he noticed that Sybil was not with her. The folding-doors were open, a lamp burned faintly in the inner room; the afternoon meal was over, and a bright fire burned in the grate.

'Miss Murray,' he said with an effort, 'is not at home?'

'Yes,' replied Michal, 'but she is in her room, resting. She has a violent headache to-day, and that is so painful an ailment with her that it necessitates perfect rest. I am very sorry.'

'So am I,' he answered. 'I wanted to speak to her.'

He was sitting in his old position by the fire-place; Michal took up a little screen, and, with her face shaded from the light, looked steadfastly at him. Then she leaned towards him and said gently,—

'Mr Vernon, you wished to speak to Sybil because you are in trouble about something. If it were possible for me to help you, I would do it gladly. I think I can guess a little of what you were going to say.'

He looked up with a start, and met the full gaze of her beautiful, solemn eyes. They were full of an infinite compassion—a yearning which he could not understand. It was like the mute appeal of some dumb creature—some mother guarding her young.

And under its influence, the icy stream of reserve and bitterness that had engulfed his manhood all these years, broke loose; he began to speak in the broken, imperfect utterance of one who feels intensely, and to whom confession is strange. And the girl sitting opposite to him, with hands rigidly clasped together, knew that the moment had come of which, in her heart, she had prophesied. 'You must be very strong,' she said to herself, sternly, and with firm lips and soulful eyes she listened.

'I have been thinking,' said the artist, in a low voice, 'that I have been dealing wrongly with you, Miss Iliff.   I think that it is incumbent upon me— that, as a just return for your kind and generous treatment—I ought to tell you something—something more—of the story of my life.   I am in a false position; not that I am arrogant enough to think that my affairs can interest either of you, but only to clear myself from a suspicion of hypocrisy.'

He spoke with a painful effort.

'Go on,' said the Poetess, very kindly.   'You are not a hypocrite, and we should never have taken you to be one, but you are right to tell us. Go on.'

'I have not spoken before,' he continued, 'because I dreaded it too much.   Your friendship has been so sweet and fresh a thing in my lonely life that I shrink from saying a word that might endanger it.   You don't know the struggle I have had to bring myself to this confession.   I am shrinking from it still.'

'And for that very reason we shall honour you the more for the victory,' said Michal, with a strong ring of sympathy in her musical voice.

'We'—the little pronoun gave him courage—he went on in a firmer tone.

'It was, perhaps, unfortunate for me that I was the

only son of a country clergyman.   My father set
his heart upon my following his own calling, and
sent me to Eton and to Oxford with that idea.   He
was a very strict man, with old-fashioned views and
prejudices, there was no sympathy between us at
all ; from the first, it seemed as though my life were
to run in untoward paths.   I hated study; I hated
the quiet parish life.   My whole energies tended towards art, and I painted in every spare moment and
picked up stray hints here and there.   And my
father, with equal fervour, opposed my bent.   Do not
misunderstand me.   I don't wish to say anything
unduly harsh of him.   He was an earnest, well-
meaning man, but there never was any accord
between us, and never could have been.   Had my
mother lived, things might have been happier ; as
it was, we simply diverged.

'It was while I was at college at Oxford that I
met the woman who was to influence all my after
life.   She was a French woman, and was boarding
with a family whom I knew.   She was many years
my senior.   I made her my divinity, and resolved
to follow art and her.   We ran away to Paris and
were married.'

The Poetess averted her face ; the look of intense
bitterness in his eyes was more than she could
bear to look upon.   He continued brokenly, the
memories that flooded his brain were an encum-

brance to rapid speech.   He fought with the words
which he wished to utter, in vain.

'I cannot,' he said at last, dejectedly, 'give you
a truthful picture of my life after the first few
months of our marriage, nor would it be meet for
me to do so.   I can only say that I had given the
best that was in me—my highest, holiest aims of
existence—to a woman whom I took to be very
little lower than the angels, and she dragged me
down to Hell—to *Hell!*' he repeated, a sudden
savage vehemence breaking through his self-control.
'You sitting there, clothed in your queenly, noble
womanhood, have no conception of the degradation
of those days.   I would not defile your presence
by the tale of what I had to undergo.   I went into
the studios and worked feverishly.   A legacy from
my godfather had made me independent, and from
my father I never heard again ; I did not expect
to, it was not likely he would forgive so vagabond
a son.   I had one ambition in the world—to work
and make a home for my beautiful wife.   In Paris,
however, that illusion was soon dispelled ; she
wanted no home of my making.   Her acquaintance
with the artistic life of Paris was far wider than my
own.   It had been gained as a model in the studios,
and the money she earned was spent, most frequently, in a drunken revel with comrades such as
suited her tastes, but not mine.   After some

months of such misery as I cannot describe to you, I made up my mind to leave it all. I returned to London to begin my life over again—I worked from that moment without ceasing, and that work saved me.'

Again silence. Michal was so still that she resembled rather a statue than a living form. The great dark eyes were fixed on the ground before her, the eyelashes did not stir.

After a spell of gloomy thought, he roused himself to continue.

'I need not weary your patience with the useless retrospect of those uncertain days,' he said sadly. 'I have never spoken of them to anyone. It is enough that they were lived through and are gone. Years afterwards I went abroad again. My health had suffered from a strain of work, and I was beginning to succeed in my profession.

'I went one spring to the Riviera—I visited Monte Carlo—it seemed to me like a peep into Paradise, and I stayed there for a fortnight in blissful content.

'One evening I wandered round the tables. I had no passion for play, and looked on from curiosity. There was a disturbance at a roulette table—a drunken woman and a man were quarrelling. Her violence was so uncontrollable that the authorities had to interfere, and as I passed

I caught a glimpse of her features. It was my wife.'

He paused. A slight shudder passed over the quiet form opposite to him, but the Poetess did not speak. He looked up and met her glance of passionate pity. He stretched out his hands towards her—a world of despairing appeal in his eyes.

'I left Monaco that evening,' he said slowly, 'and came back. I was sick of the world and of everything. I saw *that* face always in my dreams.

'To sue for divorce would always have been a thing impossible to me. To come into contact with *her* for a moment was more than I could have borne. Since then my life has been much as you see it. I have shunned society from a morbid fear of men's pity or scorn; the jealousies of professional and social life weary me; I have asked nothing of the world, save to be let alone, and it has dealt liberally with me and given me wealth and fame—but happiness, never. A man who stakes his youth and the best that is in him upon a woman who is unworthy, has lost the pearl of great price that years can never restore. So goes it everywhere in life, and men pay a heavy price for their folly.'

'And she?' Michal spoke gently, but with an

eagerness that she could not entirely control. 'What has been the sequel?'

'A madhouse,' he answered shortly. 'She has been there for some years—it is a hopeless case of insanity, brought on, I cannot but think, by the intemperance of her life; that is all.'

He threw his head back with a short and hollow laugh; the old bitter harshness had settled in his eyes.

The Poetess rose from her chair and went swiftly towards him with extended hand.

'I am very, very sorry for you,' she said simply, and the bitterness within him died.

With tender reverence, he kissed the hand she held out to him—his heart was very full.

'Poetess,' he said at last, never knowing, in his agitation, that he had used the old familiar name, 'in the waste of my ruined life I have still something left to thank God for. Can you guess what I mean? I think you can. I think your own great love can tell you how the world has looked to me since I first saw the face of your Sybil— your sunbeam—how her sweet friendship has blessed me—how it has restored to me something of the old faith—the old hope—ay, even the old happiness! It is as though a smile from heaven had come and shone upon my loneliness, making me a different man. Do you understand?'

K

She nodded silently.

'I am glad I have spoken to you instead of to her,' he went on sadly, 'for you are wise and noble, and I can leave it all in your hands. I could not go on like this, you see. You have accepted me so frankly, treated me so kindly—I could not go on loving her without letting her know it, and yet, I have no right to speak. I can make no excuses for myself, Miss Iliff. I am, as I have said, no hero, no saint. But I never break my given word, and if you tell me to go away, I will abide by your decision.'

'Stop, stop,' she cried, in an accent that was almost terror. 'It is too much to ask of me. I am not what you think—I am not so wise, so noble. To arbitrate for two lives? It is too much—too much.'

He sat silent and helpless while she moved away from him and walked restlessly up and down the room. Her proud head was thrown back, her hands clasped tightly together; he knew by the strained look in her face that she was greatly agitated, but he knew also that she was strong. Silently he waited, and watched her pass into the next room, where the little lamp was burning. She moved towards the bookcase and he saw her raise her arms slowly till her hands rested on the topmost ledge; then she leaned her head against the books, and stood there motionless.

And still he waited.

It seemed to him that he felt as a prisoner might feel when the jury had left the Court for consultation. But here there was no jury, and the judge of his destiny was that tall, dark figure standing with uplifted arms. The firelight shone with subdued brightness; he began to watch the fitful gleam of a coal that burned more fiercely than the rest. The chemistry of that coal interested him; he thought of the old primeval forests, and of all the imprisoned sunshine that is the light of civilised man. Presently he knew by the faint rustle of her gown that Michal was approaching. She came and stood before him, but he did not look up. There was a dull, reverberating sound somewhere; it seemed to echo inside his head so that he could not hear distinctly. Then he was aware of a light touch upon his shoulder, and he started up as at the sound of a command.

'Come, we will talk over it all together,' said the Poetess.

CHAPTER XV.

Judgment is given to men that they may use it.
JOHN STUART MILL.

SHE seated herself opposite to him, and he, looking straight into the earnest face, took comfort.

Her eyes were moist and full of sorrow, but the rich voice was fine and clear as a bell—not a trace of irresolution was visible in her.

'I am very glad that you have told me this,' she said with a faint smile, 'because it has been, in some sense, a relief to me. Hitherto I have not, of course, entirely understood you, and one is constrained to view with suspicion what one cannot understand.'

'I know,' he said quickly. 'I have seen that suspicion in your eyes.'

'And you cannot wonder at it!' she responded, the hot blood rushing to her olive cheek. 'Neither can you wonder when I tell you that you have asked of me a hard thing. I would rather a thousand times kill my own happiness than disturb Sybil's peace for an hour. How am I to judge in this

148

matter? I cannot. It is she who must make the decision for herself. Mr Vernon, you must come to her and tell her yourself your story.'

'Yes,' he said wearily. 'I daresay you are right, and, if you wish it, I will.'

'She is honest and true,' continued Michal, 'and unselfish; she will be as sorry for you as I am, and unwilling to cause you any further pain. For my own part, I frankly confess that I do not see why our friendship should be disturbed by this revelation. It seems to me that it should place us on a rather more satisfactory footing than before.'

'Thank you,' he said in a low voice.

The light of a sudden hope had flashed into his eyes. She saw it, and her own face grew more troubled.

'I can promise you nothing,' she went on, restlessly. 'I do not know what effect this may have upon Sybil; I only know that she has been very happy during these latter months, and that your help and kindness have been an undoubted boon.'

'I think,' he answered, with a wan smile, 'that I have had nothing to do with that happiness. It comes from within.'

'Yes,' she said earnestly, 'that is true, and you were right in calling her my sunbeam. She has always been that, and more. In childhood she was my playmate, and ever since she has been to me the expression of all that was most wonderful and beautiful in the opening years of my life. I will be frank with you, Mr Vernon, and confess that my love has not been entirely free from a stain of egotism. I had dreamt a selfish dream of our two lives being inseparable, woven together so closely that no other love should find room. I wished to shelter her myself from all the cares and troubles of this "unintelligible world," to protect her from the disturbing touch of every alien thing. I have found my inability to do this—I see that there may be wounds that even my love may not entirely heal— and the knowledge of this has been fraught with no little pain. But now, I see things differently. There are, I suppose, few soul unions free from a tinge of inequality, few absolutely reciprocal in degree and kind. I cannot fill her life as entirely as she had filled mine, and I am now content that it should be so. Our love is not the less enduring, not the less pure and true. Only, the Prince of her affection, if ever he should come into her fair young life, must be worthy of her. Believe me, Mr Vernon—rather than see her stray towards a smaller soul—Lancelot or another—I would have her lie dead at my feet!'

Vernon was silent. The passion of Medea had awakened in the depths of Michal's eyes. He noticed the likeness again, with a vague sense of wonder. Then his thought changed, and involuntarily he gave it utterance.

'She will never love unworthily,' he said with emphasis, 'neither do I think that anything in her life will surpass her love for you. But you yourself —excuse me—I am surprised, I should have thought that with your divine gift and intellectual cravings you would have yearned for a companion-ship more akin to your own mental stature. Like Mrs Browning, perhaps—another soul—'

She put out her hands with the quick gesture that he knew and could interpret.

'The thought is impossible to me,' she answered, in a low, passionate voice; 'I have always had the same feeling—that marriage would drag me down.'

She rose suddenly—her dark eyes shone with a strange light. She spoke again rapidly, resting one hand upon the mantelpiece as she stood.

'Marriage is the refuge of some souls,' she said slowly, 'the destruction of others. It is the Elysium of a few. I am thinking of it principally as it exists in European countries, under our exist-ing laws. There may come a time when—I speak as a woman, you understand?—when the sacrifice required may be lessened—when some of us will perhaps hesitate less strongly before willing to give ourselves away. I think that such a time is coming; but, however that may be, at the present time there are some lives so full of love and ambition and independence—they have carved out their own path so steadfastly—that marriage would be to them an interruption. It would mar their upward progress, and destroy their peace.'

And he knew that she spoke of herself, and was silent, while she looked down at him with earnest, shining eyes. The silence that followed was full of feeling. He had risen also, and stood before her, gazing into the flickering blaze.

'Miss Iliff,' he said gently, 'I thank you for your patience and your goodness and sympathy. I can never repay you the debt that I owe.'

'Nonsense; there is no debt,' she answered with a passing smile. 'You will come to-morrow evening and see Sybil. Then you will abide by her decision and do what you think to be right. I trust you completely. For myself, as I said, I am very, very sorry. It is not for me to blame you or to judge. I think that throughout you have been more sinned against than sinning, and for my own part, Mr Vernon, you may, if you care to do so, count upon me as your friend.'

'I think you are the noblest woman in the world,' he said impulsively—and then checked himself, fearing to offend her taste. 'I will come to-morrow, then,' he added. 'I thank you again— Good-bye.'

He left her standing there by the mantelpiece —a tall figure, upright and strong; in her eyes shone the steadfast light of friendship, on her lips a parting smile.

Bravely she stood till the door had closed upon him, and then the proud head drooped in sudden weariness, and the light in her eyes was dead.

She went upstairs and paused on the threshold of Sybil's room. There was no sound therein. She turned the handle of the door and entered.

CHAPTER XVI.

'Love is two souls and one body,
Friendship is two bodies and one soul.'

THE gas was turned down low in the burner, and, by the feeble light, she saw that Sybil was asleep. The dainty little head, 'sunning over with curls,' was turned towards the door, the long lashes lay peacefully upon her cheek. She looked very tired—very fragile—Michal's heart smote her with an overwhelming tenderness and pain. The bitterness of love consists in its inability to prevent and to conquer suffering.

For itself, it shrinks not from the furnace, but for its beloved it cries out to fate, and prays for alleviation. It becomes bold and reckless. It raises its puny arm in mad defiance against inexorable laws of the universe, and cries for a solution of the mystery of pain.

The Universe is mute; and Love, which has ever sought in vain for this solution, will seek on to the end. And there is no bitterness so deep as that of the loving soul that is brought face to face with its own powerlessness to shelter its beloved. Michal, looking down at the unconscious form of her treasure, realised this with intense grief.

'What could I do?' she said to herself earnestly. 'Surely no other course was open. To send him away were not just, not possible, and justice is the primary law. Neither could I bid him be silent, for she must know. Oh, little soul that has walked with mine so happily, would that I could keep from you the shadow of this wrong!'

Love weakened her philosophy—she could no longer reason with her accustomed self-control; she turned away from the bedside with an effort, and went downstairs.

On her way, she encountered little Miss Sally, who was making a weary ascent.

'You look tired, my dear,' said the old lady, looking with sympathetic interest into the pale face of the Poetess.

The two girls had won her heart by their thoughtfulness and courtesy, and she called them both 'my dear.'

Michal smiled back kindly.

'I do not think I am tired—I have been to look at Sybil, who has one of her bad headaches, tonight. But she is asleep now.'

Miss Sally's concern was unfeigned, and she went away, shaking her head very dolefully.

'That poor young thing is much too fragile for that crazy sort of life,' she said to herself. (Her prejudice against the artistic profession was not assuaged.) ' I do wish that artist fellow would marry her and take her out of it all, so that she wouldn't have to go toiling all day, with the smell of paint under her, nose. But there, there's no counting upon the ways of artists—they are pleasant folks enough to deal with, as it seems to me, but they want other people with ordinary heads to manage their affairs for them.'

Sybil tripped downstairs in the morning gaily, with a smile on her lips, and a song.

'Quite ready for work again, *carina?*' said the Poetess, looking searchingly into the bright young face upturned to her own.

'Oh! quite ; ripe for valour and mighty enter-prises,' laughed Sybil gaily.

The Poetess talked at breakfast-time with a show of light-heartedness.

'You will be home to tea, as usual, dear?' she said.

'Certainly ; why, Poetess, that " coming home " is the best part of the day. I don't know what I should ever do without it.'

Michal smiled. She could not bring herself to

mention the artist's name, and so Sybil was left in ignorance of his intended visit and of that of the previous night. Michal's face did not lightly betray her mind; she was grave, but self-possessed, and Sybil, the light-hearted, suspected no disturbance beneath a surface so resolute and still.

She was absent-minded, of course, but that was characteristic of her. Sybil, in her small experience, supposed that all poets were the same.

Therefore, when Michal poured the whole contents of the milk-jug into her cup, in the placid belief that it was coffee, and looked vaguely down the advertisement sheet of the newspaper in search of the foreign news, she forebore even to notice an abstraction so ordinary. She bent her sunny head over her own cup in philosophic silence.

'Dear old Poetess! She was very odd, of course, but then, she was cleverer than anybody else in the world, so what did it matter?'

Regardless of comparisons, Sybil sipped her coffee and meditated in calm content.

Leslie Vernon's visit that evening took her by surprise; he, greeting her with a nervous wistfulness which betrayed itself in his manner, saw the look of pleasure which leapt into her eyes, and regained his self-possession with an effort. Michal excused herself gently after a few minutes' desultory talk, and went upstairs to her room. She knelt by the fireside for some minutes, thinking the old anxious thoughts; but at length she roused herself, took from the book-shelf a small volume, and began to read.

The friend whom she had chosen in this hour of unrest was John Stuart Mill in his remarkable little essay on 'Liberty.' She opened it at random; its serene, impartial survey of life and life's difficulties always brought a soothing satisfaction to her mind, and to-night, as her thought travelled over the never too familiar paths, she felt this very strongly.

'Human beings,' wrote Mill, 'owe to each other help to distinguish the better from the worse, and encouragement to choose the former and avoid the latter. They should be for ever stimulating each other to increased exercise of their feelings and aims towards wise instead of foolish, elevating instead of degrading, objects and contemplations. But neither one person, nor any number of persons, is warranted in saying to another human creature of ripe years that he shall not do with his life for his own benefit what he chooses to do with it. He is the person most interested in his own well-being.'

Earnestly she endorsed the expression of philosophy, which, in its lofty endeavour to be just and unbiassed, appealed so strongly to her mind. Time flew by quickly on the wings of awakened thought and an hour had passed before she was aware.

Presently she heard the door open gently, and the book slipped from her knee. The eclectic philosophy which she had built up for her own needs was too comprehensive and deeply rooted to be easily shaken, but there are moments when all the old world's wisdom will soon faint in the passionate heat of a personal love or its complement of pain.

Such a moment had now come upon her, and she only knew that it was Sybil who had entered— that it was Sybil with bowed head and downcast eyes who had crept into her arms in silence, hiding her face on her breast.

The sunny curls strayed upward and touched the cheek of the elder girl as she bent over them. Michal held the little shrinking figure closely to her in a passionate embrace, and for a long time they remained in silence. Then the little head raised itself suddenly with a jerk, and two bright eyes looked up lovingly.

'It is all right, my Poetess,' said Sybil, shaking back her curls with a nod. 'He has told me all about it, and he has told you, too, hasn't he?'

'Yes, my darling. It was right that he should do so. And what did you say?'

The hands that were clasped round Michal's neck relaxed their hold, and were planted with desperate firmness on her shoulder.

'I said that I was very sorry for him,' she answered firmly, and that I thought he ought to try and let bygones be bygones, and go out, and be more sociable. After all, Poetess, what *is* the good of making one's self miserable if one *has* a bad wife in the madhouse? I think people ought to be kind to him and try and cheer him up, don't you?'

'Dear, little, brave girl,' said the Poetess softly, smiling a little at this serenely practical view. 'I knew that I could trust to your courage, to your sense. I would not say a word to you beforehand, because I wanted you to keep an unbiassed mind. I wanted to deal justly with you both, though I feared—very much—'

'I know,' said Sybil hastily, and as she nodded again the curls all came tumbling over her forehead until Michal put them back with a loving, gentle hand. 'I know ; but we must not always think of ourselves, and I have been trying, you see, to put myself out of it. Do you understand?'

A shadow crossed her face for an instant, but she went on bravely,—

'It seems to me, do you know, Poetess, that if you say to anyone, " I will be your friend," you are saying just the most splendid thing in the world ; and if you act up to it, you are doing the best that you could do under any circumstances. You yourself have influenced me to this belief, my Poetess. I can't see why people should ever laugh at friendship, but they do. Between two women the world does not generally believe in it, and between a man and a woman it says it is impossible. The old Greeks did not think so, did they? None of the great people, sages, philosophers, ever thought so. Somebody (I forget who) says that "friendship is two bodies and one soul," and Addison puts it before any other kind of love.'

'Yes, *carina mia*,' said Michal gravely; 'but it cannot, nevertheless, be denied that a soul-union of that kind is very rare. You see, darling, friendship grows out of the circumstances of men's lives, and life in this century and in our land is a complex thing. The love of Pylades and Orestes has not become impossible, but it is an exception; we ourselves are an exception also. Men and women of the world, so called, pass us by with a shrug and a smile, and, according to their standard, they are only consistent in doing so.' They do not understand us, for a friendship that is undying can only exist between lives whose aim is a high one—lives whose preference of higher over lower thoughts separates them from the unthinking crowd. It seems to me that this is one of the strongest incentives to nobleness that a human being can have. The nobler we are, the richer our lives will be in friendship, and love, and sympathy.'

'Yes, I know that is true,' said Sybil. 'I am sure that some people are not a bit capable of friendship, as we understand it, but I think, somehow, that Leslie Vernon would be,' she added shyly. 'Don't you, Poetess?'

She looked inquiringly into her friend's face, and being so accustomed to accept Michal's criticisms as final, she waited anxiously for her reply.

Michal smiled.

'Don't look at me like that, *carina*,' she said playfully, 'I am not an oracle to be crowned at Delphi; and seriously, I am not sure how to answer you. I do believe Leslie Vernon to be capable of all good and generous impulses—he is honest, too, as he has proved; but for the foundation of a " Platonic " friendship, which, I think, is your ideal, so much is wanted, dear—so very much—there must be equality in the affection, and—'

She hesitated, and in the silence that ensued, their thoughts lay open to each other, and were interchanged in silence.

Sybil rose to her feet with a sigh.

'My Poetess,' she said rather sadly, 'it is of no use talking; I am going to try how that friendship will work. We cannot be anything else to each other, and it would quite satisfy *me*. And, you see, dear, there is nothing else to be done, for I cannot do without him now—that is, unless I am obliged. Oh! Poetess—I am so selfish after all —I can't think why anyone should love me.'

And Michal drew the tearful little face towards her, and forgot her own sorrow in her anxiety to comfort and to soothe.

Not that her efforts were unsuccessful. Sybil lay sleeping peacefully all that night while her friend's dark eyes kept restless vigil through the long, silent hours.

CHAPTER XVII.

'If you poison us, do we not die? And if you wrong us shall we
take not revenge?'—SHAKESPEARE (*Merchant of Venice*)

'WHAT the dickens has come to Vernon?' said
Harry Travers to a fellow-artist who dropped into
his studio for a chat on one frosty December morning. 'I met him just now at Russell's, and he was
as civil as they're made—stopped me, would you
believe it, on his own account, to exchange a passing word! I have not known him so skittish in my
life before.'

The brother artist shrugged his shoulders. He
was not yet a fully-fledged member of the profession, and was inclined to look with envy and malice
upon all those of the inner circle whose crown was
already gained.

'Taken a drop too much?' he said suggestively.

'Oh! come now, that's too strong,' laughed
Travers. 'No one can suspect him of that ten-

dency. I think he must be excited at the anticipation of the triumph awaiting his new picture.
Russell has seen it, and says it's a thundering
success. If *he* says that, there's something uncommon in it, you may depend.'

'I dare say,' said the other grimly. 'It's easy
enough for a fellow with a name like Vernon's to
paint a picture that everyone will rave about. He
has time, and opportunity and cash. If he cannot
keep up his reputation, and do something decent
with that capital to back him, he must be a fool.'

'Which he certainly is not,' responded Travers.

At that moment, the subject of their discussion
was preparing for the last visit of his model, and
saying to himself, as he did so, that the Poetess
had been right.

'It should place us on a rather more satisfactory
footing than before,' she had said to him, and he,
looking back upon the four weeks that had fled so
quickly since his confession, realised the truth of
her words.

He was supremely contented; his gratitude to
her was immeasurable. She had acted up to her
promise and behaved towards him with a gentle
friendliness that was balm to his soul. The *camaraderie* established itself on a former footing, and
though his visits were purposely not more frequen
than before, yet he felt them to be more enjoyable

The bitter irony with which he had always listene
to the Christmas bells no longer awoke in h.ఎ
breast. The sunny gladness of Sybil destroyed
his pessimism, and the serious charm of the
Poetess was insensibly influencing the tenor of his
life.

The sudden entrance of his model surprised him
in a dreamy reverie. He turned immediately
with a smile.

'Ah! You have come punctually to remind me
of my last morning's work we shall get on
splendidly this frosty day—the light is really good
—for London.'

He talked cheerily while she arranged the details
of her costume and took her accustomed seat, and
then, for some time, there was silence.

She watched him curiously as he put the finish-
ing touches here and there; the portraiture was
completed, so she allowed her eyes to wander at will.

'You like that woman?' she said suddenly, and
the artist looked up.

'What? Medea? Well, you see the story I
told you about is only a story; she was not a real
person, so it does not matter much whether one
likes her or not.'

She shook her head.

'All stories are real,' she said doggedly. 'If she
was a real person, would you like her?'

'I think I might,' he answered lightly.   'She would interest me, at any rate.'

'Ah! You are not like these English,' she answered, 'cold, hard—they would call her bad—wicked.'

'Well, perhaps they would not be far out either,' he admitted, with a smile.

He found that his model had progressed so rapidly in the English language that it was no longer necessary for him to consider the form of his speech.

'Is it wicked to have revenge?' pursued the woman in a harsh voice. 'She gave much, and got back nothing—only a curse. Shall she not have revenge for it?   It is nature.'

'Nature, possibly,' replied the artist, 'but then, you see, the times are changed.   We no longer consider it a fine thing to follow Nature.   If we do, the result may be as one of our wise men has pointed out—that we may be hanged by the neck till we are dead.'

'What is that,' she said contemptuously, 'if what we want is done?'

'Humph!   I am afraid that sitting for my heroine has not improved your morals,' said Leslie Vernon.   'The vengeance of Medea is a pretty subject, but in real life her character can hardly be so pretty.   Revenge is not for human beings—it is not worth while.'

'I am not made like you,' answered the woman sullenly, and the artist, with an inward self-congratulation, went on with his work.

A little later, he threw down his brush and surveyed his picture with a long, comprehensive glance.

'It will do,' he said briefly, and turned away.

The woman descended from her seat in silence and put aside the garments of Medea.   Then she looked at the artist, hesitated, and spoke.

'I did want to ask something of the kind, signor,' she said.

'Fire away, then,' was the cheery answer, and a pair of kindly eyes smiled encouragement.

'I do live with other people of my country,' she said, 'and one is old—my grandmother. She is blind and can no more work. In England you have many houses where they do look after the old people, is it not?'

'You mean asylums, I daresay. Yes, there are many such, and also some societies for the relief of persons such as you describe.   I can find out some particulars, if you like.'

She pulled out a torn paper from her pocket and unfolded it.

'I did find this,' she continued, 'one day in a room where I sat, and they gave me this, but it is hard for me to read. It is what you call a society, and has gentlemen—see their names—at the end. They give money to old people and blind.'

The artist took the paper and glanced over it. It gave, as he expected, some information respecting a well-known charity for the relief of the aged blind.   Among the list of the patrons were several names that he knew.

'I know two of the gentlemen personally,' he said, 'but what is your object?   Do you wish to make an appeal?'

She nodded.

'I am no good,' she replied eagerly.   'I go to a great house and they turn me away.   I have no friend, and am no English.   They will not listen, but you are different.   The Earl of Trevelyan is one of the gentlemen—you do know milord?'

'Yes,' he answered, somewhat surprised.   'How do you know that?'

'I did see milord with you one evening,' she said promptly.   'That is no matter.   I did see him before.   But I want to ask him for the help for my grandmother, and if you write a little letter, signor, he would listen.'

Leslie Vernon smiled.

'You have a shrewd head,' he answered, 'and are wise in your generation.   I will help you if I can.'

He took a sheet of notepaper and began to write.

Having finished a short epistle he folded it and gave it to her.

'By-the-bye'—he paused and looked at her hesitatingly—'Lord Trevelyan is out of town and will not return before February. Had I not better address this to one of the other patrons? I could send you to Mr Dacre, with whom I am slightly acquainted, and I daresay you would fare equally well at his hands. When is the next election?'

'In August.'

'Well, you are in good time.'

She held out her hand eagerly, and took the letter.

'I will wait until milord returns,' she said decidedly. 'I thank you much, signor, for your kindness.'

'You are very welcome,' he returned pleasantly. 'I shall always be pleased to help you in any way I can.'

She stepped up to the easel and looked for some minutes in silence at the picture just completed. It interested her very much.

'I desire to see this finished,' she said, turning to Leslie Vernon, 'put in—what do you call it?—gold?'

'You mean framed,' he answered smiling. 'All right. You shall see it if you like. You had better come on my show day and see it to advantage.'

He spoke in jest, but she fixed her eyes earnestly upon him.

'What is this show day?' she asked. 'I do not understand.'

'Only one of the conventional customs of the age to which, like a flock of sheep, we submit,' he said lightly. 'On a certain day of April I invite my acquaintances to come and see me, and I show myself and my pictures to the best advantage —do you see?'

'All your friends—do they come?'

'If I have any—yes.'

'Does Milord Trevelyan come?' she persisted.

'Generally.'

She said no more, and turned away from the easel. Then she looked at him with narrowed eyelids, gravely.

'*A riverderci, signor*,' she said, and moved towards the door.

He gave her a few genial words of farewell and dismissed her; then, without another glance at the picture, he went out. He wanted to shake himself free of the '*corvée*,' which had been more or less weighing upon him since first the subject presented itself to his mind. He was very sensitive —very conscientious in his work—and, now that his mind had relaxed its tension, he breathed more freely. He was not, as has been said, great in his own self-estimate. The work that he had finished did not appear to him of unrivalled excellence ; he was too true an artist to overrate its value, but he knew that he had done his best.

He had given proof of the power that was in him. The work was vivid, impassioned, exquisite in technique ; he did not pretend to a didactic significance—it would stir the emotions, but it would not elevate the minds of men.

Yet he loved it as he had never loved any other child of his imagination ; he felt a strange impression that it was, in some way, interwoven with his future career—that he would henceforth remember it—not as a triumph of his profession, but as an episode in his life.

As he came within sight of Lord's Cricket Ground, on his way to Regent's Park, he saw the Italian woman walking swiftly along in front of him. She looked neither to right nor left, but appeared to be looking intently at something which she held in her hand. The tall figure, though partly hidden by the large shawl which she usually wrapped around her, moved with peculiar dignity. A smile played about the artist's lips as he watched his model.

' An interesting person,' he said to himself, ' but dangerous. A good model, but a bad enemy. I wonder what that little girl will have to say to the picture now that it is finished! Perhaps, next week, I might ask them to come in again.'

His eyes softened, and he straightway forgot everything in the engrossing thought of Sybil.

But the Italian woman was smiling to herself meanwhile, with a smile that was not pleasant to see.

'He is simple,' she thought to herself, whilst reviewing in her mind the conversation that had taken place in the artist's studio. 'He is simple and kind, as I said to myself on that first day. It is lucky for me that I went to him. But the grandmother!' She gave a low chuckling laugh, and a gleam of genuine amusement shone in her deep eyes. 'The grandmother!' she repeated softly.

CHAPTER XVIII.

'We are puppets, Man in his pride and Beauty fair in her flower.'
                                                    TENNYSON.

'THERE is Norah Trevelyan,' said the youngest
of a group of ladies who were taking their afternoon drive in the Park on one February afternoon.
'She looks as beautiful as ever, and as bored.'

While the speaker uttered this comment in a low
tone, a landau, bearing the Trevelyan arms, moved
slowly past, drawn by a pair of shining greys. A
bow and a smile were exchanged between the
occupants of the two carriages. Norah Trevelyan
turned to her companion and said,—

'Was not that girl pretty? You have not been
in London long enough to know her already by
sight. She is Violet Linton, who speaks so frequently, you know, at the Primose League gather-
ings and elsewhere.'

Her nephew, the young Duke of Holmsdale,
laughed merrily.

'Oh! yes, I know. She talks a lot of bosh,

that's certain. I beg your pardon, Aunt Norah. I
am sorry if she is an especial friend of yours, but
really it is true.'

Harold Fitzearse was hardly more than a boy
still—an intelligent young fellow, fresh from college,
with an open mind as yet untainted by the hollow-
ness of fashionable society, and unsullied by the
temptations incident upon his rank of life. He
was on a visit to his uncle, and, under the auspices
of Lady Trevelyan, was being initiated into the
mysteries and ceremonies of her restless little world.

'She would be flattered by your criticism,' said
Norah Trevelyan calmly. 'You are apt to be
hypercritical, Harold ; it is a pity. Real eloquence
is rare, and real genius also. When you take your
seat in the House, you will grow more tolerant.'

'You mean, I shall learn to "suffer fools
gladly?" I am not so sure. At any rate there
is one thing I will not do. I will not open my
mouth to utter a lot of rubbish on a subject which
I don't understand. That's what Lady Violet
does ; and a great many others also.'

'My dear boy, it is what everybody does, more
or less. We none of us thoroughly understand the
whole of the momentous questions of the day. It
is not in human power to grasp the whole of a
situation. We understand a little, and upon that
knowledge we speak—each for himself, according

to his angle of vision.   There are very few with brains enough and leisure enough to enable them to take a comprehensive view of the whole of a question.'

'I would rather be a specialist then, if that theory of yours were well founded,' said Harold. 'If I had not brain enough for what you call a comprehensive view, I should study the drainage question, or become an antiquarian, or something else apart from the polemical clamour of Parliamentary debate.'

'You will do nothing of the kind,' she answered. 'You owe it to your country to use your influence in a becoming manner.'

'That is, I owe it to my country to be a Tory and uphold all existing institutions, whether for good or evil.'

'You owe it, at least, to me,' she said coldly, 'not to forget that you are your uncle's guest.'

The lad coloured.   His admiration for his beautiful relative was extreme, but he could not repress a boyish love of mischief, and a certain revolutionary desire to think for himself in all things, which thoughts, moreover, were generally directly opposed to those of the majority.

'It must be a confounded bore,' he remarked, after a pause, 'to know all these people. You have bowed distinctly five times, Aunt Norah, since I last spoke. And oh! who *is* that venerable curmudgeon in the spectacles, just gone by? He is like some mouldy Don.'

'I don't know at all,' replied Lady Trevelyan still coldly; she began to find the society of her unfledged nephew somewhat embarrassing.

The lad's vivacity paled a little before her reserve; he sat in silence for a little while thinking. Then he said suddenly,—

'Aunt Norah, are you ever interested in anything, or anybody, very much?'

Then she smiled, and the parting of the exquisite lips lent a new charm to a countenance that was always, in all its moods, almost faultlessly beautiful.

'Yes,' she answered, 'I suppose I am. There are so many things in which one is obliged to take an interest, sometimes almost against one's will.'

'Ah! yes, but those things do not really interest you. You never get excited about anything— never enthusiastic.'

She laughed lightly.

'I hope not. It would hardly be my *rôle* to appear in Society like an exuberant child intoxicated with the novel delight of its first party. Besides, it is inevitable that one must outgrow such youthful enthusiasm, even if it ever existed.'

She was looking away from him now, across the restless scene before them with its prancing horses, its gay carriages, its fashionable men and women of the world. An echo of her life expressed itself in that far-away glance of her lovely eyes; a dissatisfied, even wistful, look had settled there.

'*Tout passe, tout lasse, tout casse,*' she was saying to herself—it was the key-note of her philosophy.

The young Bulgarian ambassador, who was one of her most devoted admirers, saluted her as he rode by; she returned his greeting with her usual high-bred courtesy, and the mask that was so nearly Nature slipped back into its accustomed place as before.

They drove home in comparative silence. That afternoon brought an unusual lull in the ceaseless round of social claims which engrossed the time and talents of Lady Trevelyan, and Harold enjoyed the rare experience of a quiet tea in the beautiful apartments of his hostess. He lay back in a softly-cushioned chair, and looked round with a lazy satisfaction at the amber-satin walls, the graceful furniture and the Sévres cup which he held in his hand; and, above all, at the exquisite form of the Countess, clad in its well-fitting gown of dark blue cloth, with silver-fox trimmings. But the lull was of short duration; the days that followed were marked by no such respite from the toils and delights of the gay world.

March had come in like a lamb, and the first

drawing-room passed off with success under the fair auspices of a sunny sky. Lunches, receptions and balls followed in quick succession; Harold danced with the best, and made his own naïve comments. He was a little reticent with some of the ladies who talked to him so pleasantly; his newly-acquired title sat uneasily upon his shrewd young head, like a father's hat upon the curly locks of his seven-year-old son. But the life then opened out before him was full of novelty, and altogether he enjoyed the changing scene.

It was towards the end of his visit that he accompanied Lord Trevelyan one morning to the Foreign Office, and returned alone. The east wind blew sharply in his eyes as he turned in through the gates of Trevelyan House, and he bent his head against its penetrating cold. It was not until he had ascended the few steps that led up to the entrance door, that he noticed a woman standing there, also waiting for admission. He looked at her with frank curiosity which marked his attitude towards life in general, and said pleasantly,—

' Whom do you wish to see ? '

The gleaming eyes returned his gaze with interest.

' La Comtessa Trevelyan,' she answered, showing, from under her thick shawl, the edge of an envelope. ' I have a letter for her, and must wait for answer.'

'But she is out; I am afraid she will not be home till after luncheon.'

'I will wait, if you please, signor,' said the woman.

And they entered the hall together.

The man-servant threw a suspicious glance at the strange figure as he closed the door after them, but Harold Fitzearse shared neither the distrust nor the regard for *les convenances*. He looked round the big hall, and hesitated.

'It is rather cold here,' he said, 'in spite of the fire.'

The woman nodded, and drew her shawl more closely round her.

'You had better come and wait in the library,' said the lad, and she followed him as he led the way thither.

There was a bright little fire burning in the grate; the red morocco chairs looked comfortable and warm—the uninvited guest took instant possession of one of these, and smiled.

'That is good,' she said with emphasis. 'I wait here—I thank you, signor.'

He closed the door and left her, thinking that she had the most remarkably white teeth that he had ever seen, and then dismissed her from his mind altogether.

But when, after waiting half an hour for Lord

Trevelyan, who did not return, he sat down to a solitary luncheon, his thoughts reverted to the dark-eyed woman sitting so patiently in the red morocco chair.

He glanced at the dainty dishes before him, and at the face of the man-servant in waiting. He was somewhat relieved to find that the dignified Mr Stanton was not present, but only a younger and less important member of the Earl's retinue.

'Vickers,' he said suddenly, 'I think that woman in the library must want some lunch. Will you take this in to her, please?'

Mr Vickers took the plate with a comical mixture of deference and surprise. He entered the library slowly, and cast a sorrowful glance at the savoury *fricassée de poulets* upon the tray which he held. It grieved him to serve a foreign nobody with so patrician a fare.

'His Grace desires that you have some luncheon,' he observed, as he set the plate down upon the table. The woman looked at him with a peculiar glance, and made no reply. But when he left the room, she gave a low, chuckling laugh and drew her chair to the table with a look of peculiar satisfaction, almost of triumph, in her eyes.

As the silver-toned clock upon the mantelpiece struck half-past three, Norah Trevelyan entered the library. She wore the dark blue gown which suited her figure so perfectly, and a large velvet hat with drooping feathers made a fitting frame for her gleaming golden hair. Her eyes sought those of the Italian woman a little curiously as she advanced towards her with that cold and dignified manner which served to heighten the immeasurable distance between the two.

The Italian suddenly rose and stood facing her. The colour in her dark olive cheek had deepened; the hand that still clutched the envelope moved convulsively upon her breast.

'What do you want with me?' said Nora Trevelyan.

'I want to speak with you,' said the woman hoarsely; 'to say to you what must be said. I have a letter for you, Comtessa Trevelyan.'

'Yes! Then will you give it to me, if you please,' said the Countess coldly.

The Italian controlled herself by a courageous effort, and resumed her seat.

'I pray you, my lady, to have patience,' she said in a quieter tone, 'for I am yet slow in your speech, and I have much for to say. Comtessa, I am in your country since eighteen months—I came from Italy to find you and my lord. I came with this letter for you. It is written many years—you will see.'

She extended her hand suddenly. Lady Tre-

velyan took the letter without a word, and unfolded the faded paper somewhat carelessly.

Then she asked,—

'Who sent you?'

'Read, Comtessa,' was the reply.

The note of suppressed passion in the words
struck the Countess unpleasantly. She smoothed
the crinkled paper and read.

CHAPTER XIX.

I am too forlorn, too shaken, my own weakness fools
My judgment, and my spirit whirls,
Moved from beneath with doubt and fear.—TENNYSON.

THERE ensued a silence, broken only by the ticking
of the large clock upon the mantelpiece, while
Lady Trevelyan stood upright and motionless,
scanning the faded manuscript in her hand. The
eyes of the Italian woman were fixed upon her
with a gleam like that of a tigress waiting for its
prey; she was watching her with an intensity that
could overlook no smallest detail. She saw the
delicate face change colour as her eye fell upon
the first few lines; she saw the arching eyebrows
contract and quiver, the proud lips straighten into
a rigid line. And as she saw, she smiled a smile
of triumphant malice; she knew that the proud
patrician woman before her was suffering, in a
slight degree, what she herself had suffered, and the
knowledge filled her with a terrible, savage joy.

Meanwhile, Norah Trevelyan, underneath her

mask of marble, was struggling with a vague and
threatening horror that had started up—serpent-
like—from the abyss of the unknown past. It
came upon her so suddenly—it numbed her faculties—she read and re-read the lines, but they
ceased to convey to her any meaning.

The fierce eyes of the Italian woman seemed to
pierce her very soul.

She looked up blankly from the manuscript and
met their steadfast gaze; then, suddenly, she regained her courage.

The blood of a kingly race was in her veins;
the blood of the strong and the brave. Was it
possible that she, the descendant of that illustrious
ancestry, could be so easily cowed by an illiterate
—perhaps insane—foreigner?

She held out the letter with that calm, con-
temptuous smile that is, of all things, the most
galling to a passionate nature.

'The letter is a forgery,' she said. The Italian
rose again from her chair. She understood the
phrase imperfectly. '*E falsita*,' repeated Norah
Trevelyan.

The dark eyes shot fire.

'*Falsita!*' she cried passsionately. 'Ah! see
here then. What do you say?'

She drew a ring from her bosom, and thrust it
into the Countess's unwilling hand.

Again the marble face blanched; the shot had struck home. It was a signet ring, and engraved upon the stone were the unmistakable arms of the Earls of Trevelyan.

Yet she gathered together her weakened energies with the same courage as before. Seeing that subterfuge or denial would be useless, she set herself to pluck out the heart of this mystery with her own proud hands.

'From whom did you obtain this ring?' she said slowly, shrinking a little as she anticipated the reply.

'From Howard Avory, Earl of Trevelyan,' answered the Italian, slowly and emphatically, 'the year we were married—it is now long—twenty—four and twenty years. He was young, Comtessa, and I was young, and we were married in Florence. For a little—some months—it was well, ah! very well, then he must go to England, and that letter come to me. Yes. Lucia Safrana, the contadina, is forgotten, thrown out, away, like a flower! In England are the great ladies, the big houses where they turn away Lucia at the door! *Ben!* Lucia has waited this long time to get money and to learn your speech, and she has followed milord to his big house, and has found him.'

She folded her arms and stood silent. Norah Trevelyan shrank before the fierce, determined gaze.

'I do not see what all this has to do with me,' she said evasively. 'I am not responsible for the follies which my husband may have committed when a boy. I know nothing of all this history, and have never heard your name. I am not responsible.'

She was, in reality, trying to deceive herself, trying to believe that this tale was a lie. She felt so powerless before the horror of it; it could not, must not be true. With failing heart she repeated to herself mechanically, 'Not married, never married, it is false, false, false!' And yet, in her heart lingered a terrible, unspoken fear.

'It is nothing to the Comtessa that milord does forget Lucia? *Ebbenè*, that is nature—but is it nothing that Lucia does not forget milord? She —the contadinella—is also the Comtessa Trevelyan. Perhaps milord will find a memory for that!'

The Countess turned upon her with the anger of despair.

'I will not believe it,' she said coldly. 'He *never* married you. Good heaven! it is too ridiculous. A young man of his rank may forget for a few months that *noblesse oblige*—he may be wild and reckless, he may make grave mistakes, but not to that extent. He could not have married you. I will hear no more.'

She moved away, but the woman threw herself—a determined, threatening barrier—against the door, with one hand covering the bell-handle. The Countess shrank back involuntarily, a world of scorn and displeasure in her eyes.

But the Italian was undaunted.

'You believe not?' she said. Her voice had sunk into a hoarse whisper—her gaze was resolute and stern. 'But you *shall* believe, Comtessa; you shall ask milord. Have no fear. My time of revenge is not yet—it will come, but you are safe from Lucia.'

A look of intense malice overshadowed her face.

'Yes, it will come—the revenge. Ask of Signor Leslie Vernon the story of Medea.'

She gave a low laugh.

The haughty disdain in Norah Trevelyan's countenance gave place to a sudden bewilderment as she heard the last words.

'What have you to do with Mr Vernon?' she asked.

The Italian laughed again.

'He has been a good friend, and did help me. See the eighteen months in this country I have sat as model—I find Signor Vernon one evening walking with the Earl of Trevelyan. I follow, and I go to Signor Vernon. He paints a big picture and he make me as Medea. It is a big, beautiful picture. On the show day the Comtessa will see! Then I come to this house to see milord, and they turn me away. I ask Mr Vernon to write for me a letter to milord to help my old grandmother. That was nothing—there is not a grandmother, but the letter might be good. But then I came again and see the young boy who is kind, and I think it is the Comtessa first who I will see. *Ecco!* I am come now here. They have thought me dead. Milord thought me dead, but—'

'Are you sure of that?' Norah Trevelyan stepped in upon the broken phrase with abrupt eagerness. '*Why* does he think you dead?'

She passed her left hand slowly across her brow —it seemed to her that some mocking fiend had indeed arisen from Hades to torment her.

'Why does he think you dead?' she said impatiently.

'The English gentleman, he that took my child, the little Michal, would say to him that I was dead. They all said I was dying, but after long time I got well.'

Norah Trevelyan was looking straight in front of her, with dull, unseeing eyes.

'A child—Michal,' she repeated vaguely. 'A child!'

She was growing faint and dizzy under the

weight of this oppressive tale. She put out her hand to steady herself, and her fingers closed round the carved rail of an oaken chair. Vague ideas were chasing each other across her weary brain—visions of a son and heir to the Trevelyan estates—the son for whom she herself had hoped in vain—not the child of a beggar woman, a foreigner, a savage.

The fierce eyes of the Italian were still fixed upon her.

She saw, as in a dream, the gleaming white of her teeth as the lips parted in a smile.

She tried to say something, but the words would not obey her enfeebled will. The objects in the room were moving round her; she swayed and fell forward at the Italian woman's feet.

Some time afterwards they found her lying there, insensible and alone.

.   .   .   .

It was the night of the Prime Minister's ball, but the fair, golden head of Norah Trevelyan was not visible among the guests; she was absent on the plea of indisposition. The younger beauties of the season were inwardly much rejoiced at this intelligence, which was hailed with universal surprise, for Norah Trevelyan was seldom known to be ailing, and many of the guests had seen her driving that very afternoon.

But report for once did not greatly err. The unemotional, undemonstrative nature of the Countess had given way suddenly before the unexpected assault upon her nerves. She lay all the evening upon her sofa in a restless, irritable mood ; her women came about her, but she refused their ministrations, saying curtly that she wished to be alone. So they left her—a richly-dressed, beautiful and unhappy woman in the midst of her luxurious world.

Over and over again she thought of the Italian's story in all its hateful details ; again and again she asked herself if it could possibly be true. Her thought lingered over the seventeen years of her married life—not with any emotion, for her husband had never been to her other than a necessary factor in her proud, social career. Yet her thought dwelt with approval upon him. She knew that he had fulfilled the requirements of his station better than most of the other noblemen whom she knew ; he had no vices, he was proud, courteous, even-tempered ; she had nothing to complain of in her relationship with the Earl.

And it was just this peculiarity in him—just this freedom from the vices and follies of his environment—that made her boast and her pride.

She herself had a haughty self-respect mingling with her complacency ; she had ever successfully striven to keep her fair name unsullied, her reputation beyond reproach. Women less sensitive to scandal hated her for her cold disdain, her unimpeachable propriety; men shrugged their shoulders and said that she had no heart.

But now, in her distress, she suffered as none of them would have believed it possible.

Her bitterness was not so much directed towards her husband as towards the woman who had so inopportunely emerged from the obscure grave in which she was supposed to be buried. She was inclined to make excuses for the man whom she had ever believed to be the soul of honour, and the idea of that secret marriage grew more and more incredible to her mind.

She would not allow herself to dwell upon the thought of it and its consequences, but she lay, with her jewelled hands pressed upon her forehead, looking out before her with terror-stricken eyes. Her little dogs, two Yorkshire terriers, leapt up upon her cushions and licked her hand to attract her sympathy, but she did not notice them and they went sadly away.

At nine o'clock she rose wearily and rang for her maid. 'I *must* know,' she said to herself. 'I cannot live with this suspense. I will see him to-morrow and find out the truth.'

Across the sleeping city, with her slender robe

of grey wrapped round her, came the Angel of the Dawn.

Lightly the sun-kissed wings rested with equal touch upon the weary and the joyful, upon the rich man and the poor; a long grey thread from her garment strayed through the green venetian blinds of the apartment where Norah Trevelyan lay with wide-open eyes.

She greeted it gladly. The pressure of a woe is felt less keenly when the world of bustle and activity returns to us with its duties and its claims.

She was glad too, when, later, the meek herald of the sun faded before the greater glory, and a few bright beams found their way into the room, throwing a shifting patch of light upon the satin wall.

She rose with alacrity. The dress that her maid brought her did not meet with her approval—she turned it impatiently away.

'Bring me a tea-gown,' she ordered. 'I shall remain in my rooms.'

The French maid, who was her most constant attendant, hazarded a remark.

'Had not madame better see the doctor?' she said.

'Certainly not; I am suffering merely from a headache. It will pass after a day's rest.'

Her cheek burned as she gave the answer. Whatever happened, she thought, she would not

lower herself in her servant's eyes.   And the maid
was forced to sink her curiosity in silence.

A heap of letters and papers lay upon the
breakfast-table in her boudoir.   On entering, the
Countess threw them all aside.   She went to her
escritoire and wrote a few lines on a sheet of
paper,—

'May I have the pleasure of your company at
afternoon tea in my rooms?'

The note was placed upon the Earl's writing-
table in the library, and the answer was brought to
her in the course of an hour.

'So sorry—I have an engagement at four-thirty,
but hope to see you for a few minutes after
luncheon.'

She read the few lines hurriedly, and with
clouded brow.   She had hailed the idea of a *tête-à-
tête* with her husband as the easiest plan which
presented itself to her mind.   In these days, such
opportunities were of infrequent occurrence, and
she had a curious fancy that an interview in her
own boudoir, such as she had planned, would give
her a sort of advantage over him.

The calm, self-possessed woman had become

strangely nervous. She distrusted herself and her own powers of self-control; she distrusted him also.

Might he not have been guilty, all these past years, of a duplicity of which she had never dreamed? Her heart swelled at the thought of it; a wall of hard, implacable resentment was growing up within her. She knew that if this woman's story should prove to be true, she herself was the victim of an irremediable injury—she—Norah Trevelyan, with her blue blood and stainless honour, her serene and lofty pride.

It was monstrous—incredible. She pressed her hands again and again to her forehead to ease her throbbing temples. She paced up and down the room in her agony, until thought itself became confused and weakened under this unwonted mental strain.

She tried to put the thing away from her as she had done on the previous day, but she could not. The Italian woman's eyes seemed to gaze at her from all the ornaments in the room; her fierce words rang in her ears perpetually. 'My time of revenge is not yet, but it will come.' Then she tried to listen to the voice of reason, which fear and excitement had almost annihilated within her. How could a woman of that class carry out any vengeance that should be able to touch her in her rank of life? How was it possible that this foreign

peasant woman should ever penetrate into the
world of which Lady Trevelyan was so prominent
a star?

She had succeeded in gaining admittance into
the house by a chance that would certainly never
occur again, and what revenge could be possible to
such a woman, save that of the ruffian or the thief?
Lady Trevelyan feared nothing in the world save
public scandal. She would have given her life
willingly to rescue her honourable name.

But then again, the fear that haunted her arose
and would not be quelled. Of what was this woman
not capable? She had shewn herself both determined and cunning. She had deceived Mr
Vernon, and obtained a letter under false pretences.
She had apparently nursed her grievance for many
years without faltering in her resolution—surely,
such strength of purpose, such unswerving ani-
mosity, would find an outlet by violence or by
stealth!

Norah Trevelyan shuddered at the remembrance,
and drew her soft silk draperies more closely around
her, as though to avoid a contaminating touch.

By one o'clock she had schooled herself into an
attitude of outward calm, and, after partaking of
some slight luncheon, she began to occupy herself
with some trifle of needlework until the promised
visit of the Earl.

CHAPTER XX.

Non domus et fundus, non æris acervus et auri,
Ægroto domini deduxit corporo febres,
Non animo curas.—HORACE.

THE suspense was soon ended.

Before three o'clock came a gentle summons at the door of her boudoir, and, with beating heart, she gave her husband greeting.

'I regret,' he said courteously, obeying her mute invitation, and availing himself of the proffered chair, 'I regret that you have been obliged to remain a prisoner on an occasion when you should have appeared at your best. I trust you are feeling better.'

His critical glance travelled quickly over her delicate figure, whose beauty was suggested, rather than hidden, by the loose folds of her gown; and resting upon the features whose loveliness, though so familiar, never faded before his eyes, sought in vain for a trace of illness. Her cheek bore an un-

197

usual flush, and her eyelids drooped a little heavily, but there was no other sign.

'I have exerted myself rather unnecessarily, perhaps, for the last few days,' she answered, 'and a tiresome headache was the price which I had to pay. I did not care to attend the ball last night, as I felt nervous—*ennuyée*, and, under the circumstances, I certainly should not have appeared at my best.'

The Earl smiled.

'I do not think that any circumstance could greatly detract from my wife's beauty,' he said in courteous accents. 'Pray, pardon the unwonted compliment.'

'Harold went with you, I suppose?' she continued, with downcast eyes, and fingers toying restlessly with an opal ring.

'Certainly; I think I have fulfilled my duty towards my sister's child, and have been, in truth, somewhat forbearing. Not that there is much to complain of in the lad. He is honest and generous. Tainted with the spirit of the age, that is all.'

'You mean the democratic spirit?'

'That is too strong a word. I can hardly associate a Fitzearse with a genuine democracy. No, it is rather the *rôle* of a Freethinker that he endeavours to assume; a sparkling, frothy revolutionism, engendered, no doubt, by the advanced tone of his set at Oxford. It is nothing more than a froth, and as such, will subside in due time.'

'It is to be hoped so,' said Norah Trevelyan, coldly, 'for his recklessness and disregard of all propriety may sometimes involve others in a disagreeable *contretemps*. Such has, indeed, been the case already—yesterday afternoon.'

She paused; the blood receding from her cheek again, left her very pale. Now that the moment had come for which she had tried to prepare herself, the courage in her shrank back from the ordeal.

'How so?' said the Earl, in accents of polite attention, and she summoned all her scattered forces, and spoke in her ordinary quiet tone.

'Only that he acted the very undesirable part of a Don Quixote, or some such mad and mythical hero, in encouraging an Italian beggar woman into the house and providing her, as I afterwards heard, with part of his own luncheon. A somewhat singular proceeding, as I think you will allow. The result was that I had an unpleasant interview with this person. She caused me a great deal of trouble and annoyance.'

Again a pause. Her voice was inflexible in its frigid accents. She was speaking slowly to gain time.

'A very remarkable story it seems to me,' observed the Earl. 'Do I understand you granted an interview to a "beggar woman"? And, if insolent, were there no servants at your command to expel an intruder? You might surely have spared yourself such annoyance.'

She bent her head in frigid assent.

'*Cela saute aux yeux*, but there were complications which I have yet to unfold. This Italian woman was supposed to be the bearer of a letter from Mr Vernon, which required an answer. I thought this strange at the moment, as Leslie Vernon is your friend, not mine; but I went immediately into the library, upon my return home, to receive the message. I found a handsome, gipsy-looking person, who produced—not a letter from Mr Vernon, but one written years ago, from yourself, and your signet ring. Her business, as I found, was more properly with you, and I am only sorry that, however inadvertently, I should have intruded myself upon your private affairs. I assure you that I had no wish to do so.'

She was speaking at random—her hands were so tightly clasped together that the rings pressed into her flesh, but she did not heed. She listened in painful suspense for the Earl's answer, with her eyes bent on the ground. She did not see that the bewildered expression of his countenance had given place to a look of agonised despair. It seemed to him that the terrible memory of his own sin had arisen, like an avenging angel, in his path—the conscience that had never really slept within him now started up anew with accusation and reproach; he could not answer. He felt at that moment that he could not act; he sat there, staring blankly at the drooping head of the woman who, in the eyes of the world, was his lawful wife. But her portrait was eclipsed by another, which his memory had vividly recalled. He had nothing but pity left for Lucia. The fierce-eyed, jealous woman who had followed him so persistently was unknown to him; instead, he remembered only a dark-eyed Italian maiden, full of the tender grace and passion of the South. He thought of her as of a wayward child for whom he had taken a passing fancy; he had loved her with the evanescent romantic affection of a boy. Such love is an attribute of boyhood—it will not wear. He could analyse it now with the calm, dispassionate criticism of a man who has made ambition his god, and success his heaven, and yet his heart smote him with a remorseful, bitter pain. It was not of the consequences of his deed that he was thinking —not of the complications which Lucia's sudden appearance might cause; it was the thought of the woman herself as he had last seen her, in her fresh, beautiful girlhood, that shamed him and

drove the speech from his lips. Norah Trevelyan,
unable to bear the unbroken stillness, raised her
head suddenly and met his strained, unseeing gaze.
Then she knew that the thing that she dreaded
had come to pass, and that her fears were realised.
Her heart grew chill, her features set in an expression of hard and implacable scorn.

'So the immaculate Earl of Trevelyan is not so
spotless, after all, as we have been wont to believe,'
she said slowly, with cutting emphasis. 'He can
no longer pose as a Saint Simon Stilites, far removed from the passions of ordinary men. Still,
we must congratulate him upon the tact and
cleverness that he has displayed in keeping his
entêtement secret.'

Her accents smote him with their piercing
irony; he dropped his head upon his hands in
silence.

'This pretty little *dénouement* doubtless comes
upon you unawares,' she continued. 'It seems
to me that, for the future, you will have to be on
your guard against similar *contretemps*. Madame
is evidently not yet accustomed to our English
civilisation, and is somewhat exaggerated in her
behaviour. Besides which, she does not appear
at present to cherish any great affection or regard
for you, but possibly there is some sad misunderstanding which it will be your privilege to heal.'

He looked up at her

'Norah,' he said earnestly, 'let me assure you—'

'Spare yourself the trouble, my lord,' she answered. 'Lies will avail us nothing.'

And in speaking, she rose from her seat and stood upright against the wall, opposite to him. A world of bitter resentment, of unutterable scorn, flashed out from her eyes upon the man in whose stainless honour she had implicitly believed.

'May I ask, my lord,' was her next question, 'what you intend to do?'

'To do?' he repeated wearily, in the voice of a man who hardly understands what is expected of him.

'Yes, to do. You are singularly distrait this afternoon. I suppose it is the sudden excitement of Madame's resurrection that has unnerved you, though it seems to me that I am the person principally concerned. I repeat—what are your plans for the future? Are you prepared to make due reparation to this—this—*lady*, and reinstate her before the world as the Countess of Trevelyan? The next ball at Sandringham would perhaps be a favourable opportunity. She would, at all events, create a sensation.'

He rose with a stern set face; he realised it all now.

'Cease,' he said bitterly, 'if you would not drive

me mad. Of course I am not prepared for anything of the kind. One sin in a lifetime involves one in a long chain of errors. I am not able to break through that chain; I can never make reparation to Lucia—God forgive me—never!'

'Very effectively spoken,' she said calmly, 'but the question is not so much that of repentance as of practical issues. You can settle the former account with a priest. In the meantime, you, of course, know that you have an heir.'

He started visibly.

'What do you mean? No, no—not a son—a girl—a daughter.'

'Indeed—and her name?'

'She was called Michal.'

'Ah!'

A shade of almost imperceptible relief passed over the marble countenance.

'And this Michal, what of her? In what manner have you disposed of your child? Does she follow in her mother's footsteps? I am really becoming interested in your story, my lord; it is like a novel.'

'Norah,' he spoke this time very quietly, with a determined effort at self-control, 'I owe it, at least, to you to be entirely candid now that this thing has come to pass. There must be no half truths, no suppression. I have erred greatly, but, during the last ten years or more, I have believed that my sin was expiated; I thought that she was dead. I pray you to listen to me while I tell you the whole tale from the beginning. I ask you as a petitioner; I deserve nothing at your hands.'

'How are the mighty fallen!' she said mockingly. 'Such penitence is indeed strange.'

Nevertheless, she sat down again, and with the same impenetrable features and averted gaze, she listened to his narration.

He told it very simply, omitting nothing, excusing nothing, and she felt instinctively that he was telling her the truth.

At the close she understood his conduct better than she had done before. Her own pride, her own ambition, helped her to realise the extent of the disenchantment which was the inevitable awakening from so mad a dream; she understood something of the struggle that he had to undergo before surrendering his wife and his duty to the claims of his position and rank.

It was characteristic of her worldly ethics that she did not blame him for his desertion of Lucia, only for his marriage with one of plebeian blood. And yet, she could not bring herself to forgive him or to think of him with any sympathy. The shock of this revelation was too sudden, the horror of it too great. Had he gambled, betted, or otherwise

run riot, she could the more easily have overlooked
the error, but a low marriage was in her eyes the
most irremediable wrong. She thought of it in the
apt expression of Tallyrand—'It was worse than
a crime: it was a blunder'—an expression eminently
suited to minds such as hers. When she spoke, it
was with the same cold emphasis.

'Then, do I understand that you mean to take
no steps in this matter? You do not contemplate
raising this woman from her obscurity to a position
which she would do her best to disgrace? That
is conceivable ; you would be mad to think otherwise ; though it is still an enigma to me how, in
your senses, you could ever have entertained the
idea. So Madame remains in obscurity ; that is, if
she will consent so to remain, We will not anticipate evils. But as regards your daughter, I foresee
other complications.'

He shook his head.

'I do not think she is aware of her parentage,'
he answered. 'I have seen her—once—at least I
am almost sure that it was she, and my name was
evidently unfamiliar to her.'

'On what occasion did you meet her?'

'We were dining at the Charlecotes some months
ago ; you were also present. Do you not remember a tall, dark girl in black, who sat next to me
at dinner?'

She made a gesture of impatience.

'I cannot remember all the strangers whom I may happen to meet,' she said.

'Ah! but this girl was striking!'

'No doubt; the product of such a complex union should naturally be of an original stamp.'

'You are brutal!' he said with sudden warmth. 'The girl whom I took to be poor Lucia's child has been brought up by respectable people, and has no common-place air. I knew her by the necklace which she was wearing, and I heard someone address her by the uncommon name of Michal. More I do not know, and do not care to know. I am weary of it all; I must have more time to think, and to see what had better be done.'

Her lip curled as she recognised his weakness.

'You have an engagement, I remember,' she said coldly. 'Pray do not let me detain you. We have had enough of retrospect for one day.'

He turned as if to go, and hesitated. Then he went up to her with outstretched hand.

'Norah,' he said in a low voice, which betrayed the effort he was making, 'will you forgive?'

'That is asking too much, my lord,' she answered, and he turned and left the room.

She stood for some moments, motionless, her beautiful figure thrown out in picturesque relief against the background of delicate blue. She stood there in the midst of her riches, her refinements and luxury, and the great stage of London life, with all its varied players, held not one soul more desolate than she. For, in this hour of her humiliation, the false gods whom she had worshipped, and would worship to the end, forsook her, and she had no friend on whose sure love she might rely.

She had sown the tares of false pride and worldliness upon the fair pathway of her life, and she was reaping, instead of the harvest of a noble womanhood, humiliation, anger and shame. She had married for wealth, for position, and her life was loveless and lonely as a wreck upon the sands. She had grown hard and unfeeling; she passed by the world's pure beauties, seeing nothing but the shadow of her discontent and eternal *ennui.* And now, the idols which she had set up were powerless to help her; with a bitter sense of loneliness she realised that it was so, and then, throwing herself upon the little couch in her boudoir, she gave way to her weakness in tears.

CHAPTER XXI.

'The thoughts of man are like the foraminifera, those
minute shells which build up the solid chalk hills. . . .
they are not shapeless dust for all that ; they are organic.'
Field and Hedgerow.—R. JEFFRIES.

ON that same afternoon Sybil sat at a small
table drawn up to the window, reading, with an
unusually solemn countenance, some of the loose
sheets of printed matter known as proofs.   She was
sitting very close to the window, to avail herself of
the quickly-failing daylight, and she was so engrossed
in her occupation that a visitor had been announced
and was approaching her before she was aware.

'What! has the mantle of the Poetess descended
also upon you, little girl?' said Leslie Vernon, as
he took a chair by her side; 'or are you develop-
ing the critical faculty, and writing scornful articles
for the press?'

'I am doing nothing of the kind,' said Sybil
proudly, as she swept the proofs into a drawer.

'But I am puzzled. This is a new phase, and
how am I to explain it?'

O

She looked doubtfully at him for an instant, and then a little, rippling smile took the corners of her mouth and curved them so that two dimples displayed themselves to the artist's keen delight.

'Shall I tell what they are?' she said in low voice, as if fearful of being overheard.

'I think it will be better for your peace to do so,' he said gravely; 'you won't be happy till you have let it out.'

She clasped her hands, laughing in pure childish glee.

'I have actually persuaded the Poetess to publish a wee book,' she said triumphantly. 'It is very wee, only a collection of short poems. She would not let me take more; but I chose them, and I am correcting the proofs! Oh! I am so proud—you can't think!'

'Pardon me, I can think,' he observed, smiling, 'for I see you visibly growing in importance under my very eyes. Good gracious! what a triumph for you! And she lets you correct her proofs, does she? Humph! are you sure you know how? Let me see a specimen.'

'I shall not,' said Sybil, with a sudden access of dignity betraying itself in the lengthening curves of her neck. 'I shall not show you anything, because you laugh. I think you are a disagreeable man.'

'*Et tu, Brute?*' he said, and became penitent. He often teased her for the fun of it ; he liked to see the laughing eyes sparkle with concentrated mischief; he liked to watch the expressive little face changing under his banter, from seriousness to laughter, from grave to gay. 'I congratulate you,' he said more earnestly. 'I do indeed. I think that anything that comes from Miss Iliff is worthy of the praise, not only of our esoteric few, but of the multitude. I am very glad.'

Sybil nodded ; her eyes were still sparkling with excitement and joy. She reopened the drawer in the table, and turned over the proofs once more.

'They will be ready soon,' she said gaily. 'Next month I expect we shall have the book.'

He drew a column or two gently from her unresisting hand, and glanced over them. He would have recognised the authorship, he thought, even had he not been told : there was a strength, a passion in the lines he read, which reminded him powerfully of Michal. The style was classic in its simplicity ; he lingered over it in keen delight and appreciation.

'You will find henceforth that the world has a mind also to appreciate your Poetess,' he said, rather sadly. 'It will rush and buzz around her in a whirl of adulation, when some critic leads the way. Her work will no longer spread its modest perfume, unrecognised, at your sacred and solitary shrine.'

'That is as it should be,' said Sybil, with a bright, sweet smile. 'I know her and love her, and have her always. The world should know her, too. It could never rob me, you see, of my special triumph.'

'No,' he returned thoughtfully. 'It could not do that, and she herself, in her passionate altruism, is not made to shine in a narrow sphere. This work that she has done is but a beginning, an earnest of what she will do hereafter.'

Sybil gave him a grateful look. She knew that his reverence for the genius and character of Michal was genuine and intense; she knew that her friend's influence had become potent with him, and she rejoiced that it was so.

The artist turned again to the poem that had attracted his attention. Michal entered quietly, while he was still reading it, and greeted him with a look of grave surprise.

'Forgive me,' he said rising, with one hand still covering the proofs. 'I came upon Miss Murray unawares in her labour of love, and the love so far outshone the labour that she was forced to betray herself, and so I became a partaker in her too transparent secret.'

'You plucked out the heart of the mystery,' said the Poetess smiling, 'and found therein—'

He intercepted her, and turned the phrase to his liking.

'I found therein a gem,' he said gravely, 'which will be set in the succeeding ages in the hearts and minds of men. Don't misunderstand me. I could not offer you compliments. I have only spoken the thought as it came.'

She moved away and knelt down by Sybil's side. When she spoke, it was in a voice that trembled slightly.

'Perhaps over-sensitiveness is a quality with which most poets are encumbered,' she said. 'I am afraid that I am endowed with a considerable share.'

'All workers must be more or less susceptible,' replied the artist, 'if their standard is high.'

'Yes, but all have not the same responsibility,' she answered, and paused, feeling at that moment the inadequacy of speech. 'Thought is such a marvellous thing,' she said slowly, after a few minutes' silence. 'It springs from eternity, and is yet as young as Time. It is born with every second of our existence; it flashes out before us from the eyes of little children, from the cosmic process, from the wonder and mystery of Life. Who shall sow it and who shall gather? We cannot tell whither it comes or goes. Only we are responsible for these immortal offspring sent out into the world—these small, winged thoughts, which we shape to our liking, are the deathless inheritance of the ages, far removed from the decaying grasp of Time. The poet dies and is forgotten, but his white-winged thoughts endure for ever in some form, old or new.'

'It is curious,' said the artist thoughtfully, 'to reflect upon the large number of persons in whom lower and baser thoughts habitually predominate. How is it? Is it some defect in their mental vision? To try and raise such a mind from its low level is utterly fruitless. You might as well try to raise one of the rude pillars of Stonehenge.'

A trace of bitterness had come into his voice. Sybil's eyes sought his in a fleeting glance of sympathy.

'I suppose that some have a natural bias—call it hereditary until otherwise proved—that leads them to such a choice,' said the Poetess. 'Then there is the bias of education and other influences which surround the individual life. It seems to me that what we call an intellectual life is one in which the higher thoughts predominate over the lower. It is something altogether apart from cleverness or wit; it is within the grasp of us all.'

'Ah! I like that idea,' he said, smiling. 'It is so extensive; for the working-man in all countries may live an intellectual life at that rate, even though he be possessed of the most fragmentary knowledge.'

'Just so,' answered the Poetess earnestly. 'At least, that is a theory of my own, and therefore open to correction.'

'But there still must be degrees of intellectual capacity, must there not?' said Sybil shyly. 'There seem to be a few who are singled out as torchbearers, whose example tends to strengthen the others who find their journey difficult and long.'

The artist smiled back at the happy little face as he answered.

'Most assuredly I believe in our "torchbearers" as heaven-sent messengers of good. And I believe, also, that it is principally in the crowded highways of life that we find them, not in the backwoods of solitude.' He met a slightly inquiring glance from Michal, and continued warmly,—'No, I do *not* believe in solitude; I think that it is in the midst of our varied humanity, and from the sympathies generated by such intercourse, that the noblest lives are formed. You smile, both of you. You think that I do not practise what I preach; I remind you, possibly, of Carlyle "talking for four hours in praise of silence," but you must not condemn me too soon. See, though I have lived practically alone all these years, yet I have lived in

London. I have gone out at all times into the great "hive" of the city, and have seen its men and women wrestling with all conditions of life. I have watched them now and then. I have come in close contact with them. Ah! the pathos of life: the grim irony of it down in that nether world! Then I have, at rare intervals, accompanied Trevelyan into the flowery courtyard of his higher sphere; there was life again, but how different! No longer the ache and the struggle to be seen through weary eyes—only a mask of honied smiles and a polish that defied detection. And this is our "idol ceremony"—this our civilisation! I have come home at night to my lonely room, and thanked God that I did not lead the life of those men and women. My acquaintances misunderstood me; they thought me hard, unfeeling, cold; but it did not matter. They could never understand that I craved only the sympathy of a kindred soul—only one soul to love!'

He checked himself suddenly; in his scrupulous desire to avoid the slightest expression of the love that was in him, he habitually shunned all personal talk. But now he had been thoughtlessly carried beyond his limit, he turned the conversation swiftly back to a point whence it had been diverged.

'So, you see, I look upon solitude as a restorative,'

he said, 'and not as a wholesome, everyday fare. I believe that you both agree with me.'

'Yes,' answered Michal, 'speaking only for ourselves, for I think it is a question of individual taste and necessity. To some minds, a long period of absolute quiet is now and then essential—others can be satisfied with less.'

Sybil's hand was resting upon her shoulder—she took it gently in her own.

'This is a very sociable little person,' she said with a quiet smile. 'No penchant for nunneries and retreats in this quarter—no relish for solitary walks "far from the madding crowd."'

'Certainly not, when they lead into bogs and horrid places where people get lost,' was the irreverent reply. 'I don't go star-gazing all over the country and get my feet wet, and lose myself, but I know some people who do.'

'What do you think of that for a *reducto ad absurdum ?*' said the artist, with a grim amusement betraying itself in the corners of his mouth.

'I shall say with Mercutio,' answered the Poetess, laughing—'"Come between us, good Benvolio; my wit faints."'

'I don't know what Benvolio might have thought, but I prefer to stand on neutral ground,' said Leslie Vernon.

CHAPTER XXII

'Post eduitem sidet atra cura.'

IN sweet converse they lingered while the shades of twilight fell, until Sybil's sunny head showed faintly against the window pane, and the stately figure of the Poetess stood out like some darkened statue amidst the surrounding gloom.

Very precious was this hour to all of them; under its mystic influence their talk grew serious and calm. The stirring animation of the dawn, the impassioned life of the noontide, had faded, and tranquil thoughts, with graver meditations blended, stole in upon the failing of the day.

From the current events and interests of the time their talk wandered away to other themes; skimming here and there some subject with light, indifferent touch, and probing others with the earnest spirit of inquiry that besets thoughtful minds. These talks were felt by each of them to

be very helpful, exhilarating, free.   Philosophy
and fancy breaking through the bands of everyday
reserve, flowed in eager, impassioned music from
the lips of Michal; and the others, with scarcely less
enthusiasm, followed her daring lead.   All that
was best and noblest in Leslie Vernon sprang forth
at these moments into activity; the veil of cynicism, through which he had been wont to look at
the universe, dropped away before the softening
influence of these two fair and earnest lives.   He
had always enjoyed the society of women; even the
wreck of his married happiness had not spoilt his
appreciation of their refinement and beauty, nor
destroyed his reverence for the sex; and now such
reverence was placed upon a firmer footing, and he
was free to enjoy the sweet companionship as he
had never been before.

His manner had become of late insensibly
softened, and his laugh, so rarely heard in the solitude of his home life, rang out with the light-
hearted spontaneity of youth.   But this evening
he was especially grave, and a slight sadness, for
which he could not account, manifested itself in his
voice and conversation, and when he rose to take
his departure, it was with a sense of desolation
which he endeavoured to crush down.

'Sir, we have had a good talk!' said Michal
brightly, as their hands met in a grasp of friendly

goodwill, and, with a smile at the apposite quotation, he went out into the night.

The studio, when he re-entered it, was but faintly
illuminated by the glow of the street lamp outside,
and he did not desire any further illumination.

He went slowly across to his accustomed chair,
and sat down.

For the first time for many weeks he felt inclined
to murmur at fortune's dealings with him; the
happiness of those evening visits, the luxury of the
sweet companionship made the loneliness of his
life more apparent still. It was good to have such
companionship, to enjoy such rare communion of
soul; but it was a desolate thing to come home
again to a hearth unhallowed by the presence which
he loved, but could not perpetually enjoy. He
knit his brows as his thoughts flew back to the
early days of his career, and the fatal error that had
blighted all his youth. What an awful thing it
seemed to pay so heavy a price for an act, not of
sin, but of foolishness! His despair rose up in
intense revolt against the laws which handicapped
his freedom; he cursed the hot-headed impulse of
his boyhood, and the character of the woman to
whom he was irrevocably bound. *Irrevocably
bound!* In realising the closeness of the tie, he
shuddered. 'A helpmeet!' he said to himself, with
terrible irony; 'a life companionship whose love

surpasses time!' That was what men thought of when they married ; that was the ideal of marriage ; the actual experience of a few. It had been his ideal also ; the instincts of home and domesticity were largely developed in his character, but the experience !—

So strongly did the old, painful memories arise within him that he started up with a sudden desperate resolution to shake himself free and to turn his thoughts back into a happier channel.

The morbid bitterness which he had formerly been somewhat apt to foster, now settled rarely upon his thoughts; he threw off the gloomy retrospect with a strong effort and took up a book to read.

The morning dawned fair, with a slight breeze blowing from eastward, and bright gleams of sunshine, with promise of the spring.

At eleven o'clock the artist was walking briskly down Pall Mall, striding along with an easy pace habitual to him, and the 'ragged staff,' as usual swinging in his hand.

As he neared the Carlton, his eye fell upon a brougham with a pair of bays standing outside the door. He recognised it at once, and halted.

At that moment the door of the club opened and Lord Trevelyan came out towards him; he returned the artist's greeting hastily and with a somewhat abstracted air.

'Whither bound, my lord?' said Leslie Vernon, taking in at a glance the grave look of preoccupation that clouded the weary eyes of his friend.

'Home,' said the Earl briefly. Then, with a sudden change of manner,—'Are you walking my way? Come with me, then. I have an appointment at twelve, but we shall be in time.'

He dismissed the carriage without waiting for an answer, and the two men walked for some minutes in silence over the familiar ground.

'You look remarkably self-satisfied, Vernon,' said the Earl, glancing at the artist's face, with its grave but interested scrutiny of the streets and the passers-by.

'It is your depression, my lord, which resents my cheerfulness as an insult. The world, I am afraid, does not at the present moment appear to you in the gayest of colours.'

'It is a blockhead of a world, in truth,' said the Earl lightly, 'but I am not so much disposed to quarrel with it. It serves our purpose well enough if we have only the sense to avoid its pitfalls.'

'Ha! you would place common sense—the philosophy of the uncultured—at the head of our human attributes,' said the artist smiling. 'I am glad you are inclined to do justice to so plebeian a quality.'

'Nothing so rare can be called plebeian,' answered the Earl gravely. 'Common sense appears to me to be the unknown quantity in most men's lives. We have talents, opportunities, fortune; and we throw them all to the devil for want of a little common sense in our management of them.'

'Most true! Indeed, we might liken the man who does not possess that divine quality to the "pair of spectacles behind which there is no eye," as Carlyle hath it.'

'Just so; only I never called it a divine quality. I should have said it was very human, like the rest of us. I don't quite see where the divinity comes in.'

'Don't you? Well, perhaps not; it often seems to me a little difficult to determine where divinity ends and humanity begins. Perhaps they are really more closely interwoven than we are generally disposed to recognise.'

'Ambiguous, indeed,' said the Earl drily. 'Have you been steeping your mind in more German poetry of late? Such an access of sentimentality is strange.'

'Sentimentality, is it? Then I apologise. Far be it from me to offend your practical English ears with undemonstrable theories or romance.'

The Earl smiled.

'Oh! it does not offend me at all; it is rather entertaining. The majority of men are not at all amusing; I like your idiosyncrasies by way of a change.'

'Thank you.'

The artist suddenly halted to say a few words to an Italian organ grinder, who was apparently an old friend. After a few minutes of animated conversation, and gesticulation on the part of the monkey who accompanied the machine, Leslie Vernon walked on quickly to overtake the Earl.

'Pardon my discourtesy,' he remarked with a smile. 'An old acquaintance of mine.'

'Pray do not let me detain you,' said the Earl coldly, 'if you wish to prolong the conversation. For my own part, I do not, as you know, share your penchant for beggars and tramps.'

He spoke with unusual bitterness, and the artist was irritated by the injustice of the remark.

'You do not take the trouble even to be accurate, my lord,' he answered warmly. 'That man is earning his living honourably, and is therefore no beggar. He is leading a life in every way creditable, and has as just a claim to the respect of the multitude as you and I may have.'

'Confound the multitude and their respect!' said the Earl, with asperity. 'What is their opinion

worth? Have I no title to their respect or consideration? Or is this immaculate organ-grinder
to be preferred before all the crowned heads and
nobility in Europe?'

The artist, looking in surprise at the man from
whom he had never previously heard a hasty
answer, saw that he was speaking under the influence of some painful irritation, and that he was
hardly conscious of his words.

'My lord,' he answered quietly, 'you misunderstood my meaning if you could take offence at it.
I only wished to assure you that my *protégé* is a
respectable member of society, such as you would
be the last to condemn.'

The cloud resting angrily on the Earl's brow
cleared somewhat. The windows of Trevelyan
House had become visible in front of them; he
stopped and held out his hand.

'I am not up to the mark to-day, Vernon,' he
said wearily. 'You must excuse me—I have been
a good deal bothered with business and other
things.'

The artist grasped the hand extended to him,
with one of his rare, bright smiles.

'Say no more,' he replied heartily. 'I knew
that you were oppressed by some burden—I wish
I could help you. Good-bye.'

And then he walked away, thoughtfully, saying

P

to himself, for the hundredth time, that life in Lord Trevelyan's circumstances was a very arduous and weary thing. But he did not know how weary.

Had he been able to follow the Earl into the library, where his lawyer awaited him, he might have realised how very far from the mark his sympathy had been.

An hour afterwards, the lawyer, a shrewd and capable man of business, had become acquainted with some details that surprised him greatly, but at which he was too thorough a man of the world to manifest his astonishment, and the Earl of Trevelyan, repairing once more to the solitude of his own chamber, told himself that his reparation had been made.

None could know the price, as none could ever know the struggle—the wounded pride—the violated self-love that had been offered at the shrine of his resolution. Neither did anyone know the shrinking cowardice, or the haunting fear that perpetually rushed upon him, and made the usually reserved and courteous nobleman a prey to nervous and irritable outbursts.

The knowledge of his sin had lived with him all these years in secret—the reparation would be secret, too.

So he told himself, so he tried to believe, and yet that fear!

What was it that made him start at his own shadow and shrink from the sea of unknown faces in a public hall or any crowd?   He threw himself into the interests of his life with all the energy that he could assume, but it did not help him; under all the activity his own self and its tormenting doubts and fears rose up habitually before him; black care was his constant companion, and clung to the saddle with a grip of iron.

The stately, beautiful presence of Norah Trevelyan moved in and out of his life without a word. He hardly felt her existence; he was only thankful to escape from the cutting irony of her speech, the bitter scorn of her lovely eyes.

The days went by, monotonous and dreary, though full of bustle and interest and life, and he played his part mechanically and well.

'You can always rely upon Trevelyan,' said some of his friends.

'He never breaks an appointment, and he always does what he says he will.   Honourable fellow, Trevelyan,' said the others.

'Never does anything underhand or mean.'

So they said and so they believed, and that was 'the humour of it.'

CHAPTER XXIII.

'Vive memor lethi; fugit hora.'

IT was the fourth of April, and the usually placid monotony of Leslie Vernon's quiet dwelling was disturbed from its routine.

For the first time in his life the artist was roused into a pleasant and eager anticipation of the ordeal which formerly he had disliked and despised.

He moved about with alacrity from room to room, superintending the small details of arrangement and decorations. The servants, with profound wonder, saw him bringing in large bunches of golden daffodils, which shone in masses of glorious colour against the deep blue dado of the rooms.

He arranged them himself; he took a delight in their beauty and in the simple picturesqueness of the studio which, by a skilful readjustment of its furniture and ornaments, he contrived to show at its best.

He surveyed it all at length with a gleeful satisfaction quite disproportionate to the event, and awaited the arrival of his visitors with an eagerness which he would hardly have cared to confess. It was certainly not of the critics that he was thinking; it mattered to him not a jot whether the crowds who would examine his pictures spoke of them well or ill. There had been a time when he was dependent upon the good opinion of the authorities; when a few words of public praise had been eagerly seized by him—eagerly coveted—but that time was now no more.

With tranquil indifference he accepted applause or blame, having attested each at its true value.

His elaborate preparations had not been made for the delectation of the critics; he was thinking all the time of the bright, eager eyes that would take in all the details of the studio, and whose searching glance would penetrate each nook. He was thinking, too, of the quiet pleasure that would shine in the dreamy eyes of the Poetess, and of the naïve comments that would be gathered afterwards from Sybil's merry lips. He welcomed the first few visitors with an unusual cordiality, and as the room began to fill a little, and the buzz of voices grew into a crescendo of congratulation, question and small talk, he kept constant watch upon the door. When at last he moved forward to greet the expected guests, it was with a subdued triumph and excitement in his manner that the girls at once observed. His quick, appreciative glance travelled swiftly from Sybil's delicate grey gown, with its knot of pink carnations, to the flushing cheeks and sparkling eyes that were looking with such frank curiosity around. Her nineteen summers sat so lightly upon her, the fair little face was as happy and innocent as a child's.

By her side, Michal's queenly figure and gentle dignity made the contrast, as usual, strong. Her thoughtful face wore an expression of calm serenity; the look that occasionally recalled the portrait of Medea was entirely absent now.

After a cursory examination of the few other pictures in the studio, the interest of the visitors had entirely centred round the larger and more important work. Comments and congratulation flowed freely throughout the room; the artists who were present realised the charm and power of the portrait, and gave generous praise, which mingled grotesquely with the more garrulous speech of the uninitiated.

Lord Trevelyan, who had arrived late and was unaccompanied, returned the artist's greeting with his accustomed cordiality of manner, apparently unharassed by any care. He stood for some time in silence looking at the picture of Medea.

It did not please him ; he had sufficient knowledge to enable him to appreciate the delicacy and
beauty of the technique ; but the conception did
not delight him at all.

'I should have been afraid to sit in the room
with such a person,' said a lady, glancing somewhat nervously through her eye-glasses at the
powerful face, with its fierce, dark eyes. 'Really,
I do not think it can be safe to have such models ;
one might be robbed or murdered'—and the
nervous critic hurried away to find a more con-
genial subject in a graceful study of a flower girl.

'Who is it supposed to be ?' whispered a young
girl to her non-artistic friend, as they, too, stood
in front of the large easel, and vented their criticism
in subdued tones.

'Hush ! you will hear presently,' was the cautious
answer. 'I expect it is Cleopatra, or somebody
like that, from the dress.'

Lord Trevelyan, overhearing the explanation,
glanced round at the speaker with a slightly
amused smile, and his attention was arrested by
the serious face of Sybil.

A bow and smile were exchanged between them.

'And what is your opinion ?' said the Earl.

'What ? of the picture ?' she answered.

'Oh, I think it is very beautiful indeed.'

'But that is a bald criticism.   Have you nothing

more advanced to offer?   No fault to find?   You are quite behind the age if you have none.'

She looked at him doubtfully, suspecting sarcasm, and grew shy.

'I could not criticise,' she said simply, edging away a little, so that another visitor stepped in to take her place ; and as she did so, she encountered the smiling glance of Leslie Vernon.

He was standing apart, talking to two well-known artists, and he looked remarkably bright and genial.

His acquaintances noticed it, and felt more at their ease with him than formerly, while the few who saw him for the first time were agreeably impressed by his look and manner.

Sybil wandered away on the track of the Poetess, who was thoughtfully surveying a small landscape sketch ; and as she moved, her glance travelled curiously round the studio.   With intense satisfaction it rested upon the fair head of the Aphrodite, the beautiful Roman urns and amphorae, and the gleam of the daffodil's gold.

Amid the hum of voices she could distinguish ever and anon the smooth, level tones of Lord Trevelyan.

'Mr Vernon has presented the old-world story to us,' he was saying, 'in a remarkably striking form.   He has blended myth with reality.   The

story of Medea has a significance even in our time;
it brings us face to face with the two most powerful
human attributes—love and jealousy.'

'And the sequel—hate and revenge,' said a
gentleman who was standing by. 'Yes, the story
is as old as Time. Civilisation develops and religions change, but human passions are much the
same in all lands and ages.'

At that moment some of the visitors became
aware of a slight commotion near the door of the
studio. A woman had just entered—a tall woman
with a red scarf about her head, and a shawl
enveloping her person. The group at that end of
the room, surprised at her entrance, gave way a
little, and simultaneously a murmur ran through
the room.

'The model! the model!'

'It is Medea come to life! What does this
mean?'

A cloud of strong annoyance passed over the
artist's face as he endeavoured to advance towards
the intruder; but the crowd pressed back upon
him, so that he could not immediately break
through.

With growing perplexity and embarrassment he
saw the woman make her way swiftly to the large
easel where Lord Trevelyan stood. There she
halted; her tall figure rose slightly above the heads

of the people round her; her arms were apparently folded beneath her shawl. She was speaking now in a harsh, penetrating accent that rang through the room, and the people involuntarily shrank away from her, with a vague sense of alarm.

'Milord—Lucia has come back to you,' she said slowly. 'Have you a memory for her? Ah! yes, I see you do remember, but it is too late, milord, too late.'

And she broke into a passionate torrent of Italian.

Those who saw the face of the man to whom she was speaking, remembered it to their dying day. He never spoke, he seemed hardly to understand her; he stood erect and rigid as though he were turning into stone.

With a sudden impetus of apprehension, the artist rushed forward and seized the woman by her arms—at the same moment the crowd fell back, panic-stricken; the report of a pistol echoed sharply through the rooms, and the Earl of Trevelyan lay senseless on the floor.

Sybil, faint and dizzy with the shock of an event whose full significance was not as yet revealed to her, had a confused recollection of what followed. She only knew that the visitors had assembled quickly in the tea-room, and that the greater number immediately left the house; she remembered the panic that had ensued, the confusion, the buzz of voices, and the clear, decisive tones of Leslie Vernon rising above them all.

In the midst of it all, the Italian woman was forgotten. She stood quietly by while a physician, who was among the guests, made a hasty examination of the wounded man, and, having heard the verdict, she turned and escaped unnoticed.

'Dead!' said the physician briefly, looking up into the anxious face of the artist.

Leslie Vernon turned away with a mute gesture of despair, and encountered the grave glance of Michal, who stood silent and self-possessed by his side. Instinctively he turned to her as to a friend whose counsels he valued.

'Don't go,' he said simply, and threw an inquiring glance round the empty room.

'Sybil is with a few others who are yet remaining,' she said, answering his thought.

'Yes, yes—will you go to them—offer anything —do what is right—I must stay till—'

He looked down at the face of the dead man and shuddered. The Poetess left him without a word.

The few visitors who remained forgot to see anything strange in the gentle ministrations of this tall and dignified stranger, whose gracious self-possession acted like balm upon their nerves.

They lingered to hear a few words of explanation, and soon there was absolute silence throughout the deserted rooms.

'Come, dear, we will go,' said the Poetess, and as they passed into the hall the artist met them.

'Stay one moment more,' he entreated, 'and give me the relief of talking to somebody. It is done now, they have taken him—' He waved his hand towards the empty studio. 'I cannot go in there again—it is—too awful—'

The girls followed him silently into the dining-room. He threw himself upon a chair and continued wearily.

'They have taken him home—home—and only an hour since he crossed the threshold in all the strength of his manhood and health. And I feel as if I were in some way accountable for it. I, who valued his kindness so truly, who never heard a harsh word from him, who esteemed him as a friend!'

Oh; infinite pathos of regret! In his lowly self-estimate, this man was prone to overlook the faults of others, and to esteem all men more worthy than himself : and now, when the friend whom he thus honoured was taken from him, he remembered nothing save his virtues.

'And Lady Trevelyan,' said Sybil in wide-eyed distress. 'How dreadful for her, too.'

'They have telegraphed to her,' he replied.

'She was away for a day or two. Yes, it is all a mystery; I can't read it. Perhaps the secret will for ever remain unknown; but, whatever it may be, it could not alter my feeling for Trevelyan. I must speak of him as I found him, as I knew him always.'

'But the woman?' said Michal gently. 'Is she gone?'

'Yes; made her way out, somehow, unnoticed; the police will be soon on the track, possibly they will find her. For my own part, I hope they will not succeed. It seems to me a poor satisfaction, the taking of a life for a life destroyed. It was the code of the old Judaic law which Christianity opposed, and has as yet opposed in vain. If the woman is found, we may know more of her story and of her wrongs. Wrongs there must have been, but she has revenged them. "After life's fitful fever he sleeps well." Nothing can alter that— nothing can awaken him.'

Michal's face was very troubled. Sybil, by her side, wept silently.

'How did she come in?' asked the Poetess; 'did you expect her?'

'Certainly not, but the servants have seen her so often, they did not think of refusing her when she asked to be allowed to wait until I might be at liberty. She was shown into the little room at the back of the dining-room, from thence she made her way into the studio easily enough. I remember telling her some time ago that my show day would be on the fourth. I told her unthinkingly. I had no suspicion.'

'Was she mad, do you think?' asked Michal.

'No, she was not mad. I feel convinced she was sane. She had shown herself all through to be capable of a silent and consistent cunning. Had I but guessed! Had I but known!'

A few minutes later the girls rose and left him. There was nothing more to be said—nothing that could be done. The shock was too great, too sudden to be mitigated as yet by many words and sympathy. Time alone could remove the horror of the remembrance, and they left him alone with his sorrow.

Early the following week the artist paid an afternoon visit to the house in Maida Vale. He was taken by surprise when Sybil came forward to give him greeting.

'I did not expect to see you,' he said. 'I have come, as usual, to beg for something. This time, for help from your Poetess, as my own wits are in fault. Is she at home?'

He took a seat, and then, looking at her, noticed for the first time the traces of strong agitation in the sweet, serious eyes.

'Michal will be here directly,' she answered, and then paused, as though expecting him to speak again.

'Is she not well?' he said anxiously. 'Has anything gone wrong with you? What new untoward circumstance can have arisen to trouble your peace? I see there must be something.'

'Oh, yes! At least, not exactly wrong to us, only it is all so strange—so upsetting. Change is always unpleasant when one is very happy.'

She paused again; explanation was evidently difficult to her.

'Does the "change" concern Miss Iliff?' he asked again.

There was a strong ring of anxiety in his voice. His recent experiences had led him to be a little apprehensive of other ills.

Sybil moved restlessly away, and answered with a great effort,—

'Yes, it concerns the Poetess. You must not call her Miss Iliff; she is not Miss Iliff at all. Oh, dear! it is all so strange. We never knew her father's name, you see; and who would ever have guessed anything about Lord Trevelyan? Who would have suspected for a minute that that furious Italian woman was his wife? Oh! it is all very horrid! And, forgive me, Mr Vernon, your friend was a bad, wicked man.'

The artist stared in helpless stupefaction as this revelation was thus disjointedly unfolded before his inquiring mind, and his gaze remained fixed upon the serious little face before him, flashing with such righteous anger and scorn.

He did not take in the full meaning of her words. How should he, when the story of Michal's parentage had never been revealed to him? He only repeated to himself mechanically,—

'A bad, wicked man—Lord Trevelyan!'

The words conveyed to him no meaning. Again, he shook his head—he could not understand it at all.

CHAPTER XXIV.

'I would have seen thee sooner, Italy,
For I have heard thee crying through my life.'
E. B. BROWNING.

AFTER a pause, the artist began again slowly,—

'Then—do I understand that Miss Iliff is—?'

'She is Lady Michal Avory,' said Sybil, with some sharpness. 'And if he—her father—had behaved like an honest man, instead of a weak coward, we should all have known that long ago.'

She spoke impatiently. The events of the last week had been very distressing to her, interrupting, as they did, the even tenor of her happy life, bringing her face to face with problems and errors which before she could but dimly realise.

Her bright, fresh mind looked out upon these things with sorrow and recoil; where the Poetess acted, she could only feel, and she had felt these recent troubles intensely.

In the silence that followed, a light dawned upon Leslie Vernon, by whose illumination he saw many

Q

things as they had never appeared to him before, by which also some mysteries became clear to him, some crooked things straight.

He rose silently as the Poetess entered : in his look there shone a mingled feeling of reverence and compassion. But the words died upon his lips as she came forward ; the tall figure looked all the statelier, in its simple, velvet gown ; the face, with its solemn eyes, seemed all the graver, sweeter, holier, for its impress of conquered pain.

'I am glad to see you,' she said simply, 'on whatever errand you have come. Please sit down again.'

But he took no heed and remained standing before her chair.

'I am come to ask your aid,' he said slowly, 'but I can hardly venture to do so now. I had expected and hoped to find a peaceful household apart from the storms of life ; I am indeed grieved to find it otherwise.'

'Sybil has told you, then ?'

'Just a few words—an outline merely of the facts. I can hardly believe it. I do not understand it—as yet—'

He saw the look of pain in her eyes and was silent.

Gently she endeavoured to turn his thoughts back to the consideration of his own affairs.

'I should like to know in what way I could aid you?' she said.

He drew a letter from his pocket, still hesitating.

'I do not like to trouble you,' he answered. 'It may cause you further pain; it is an Italian letter which I have received, and I was going to ask you to interpret it for me.'

She held out her hand eagerly.

'Italian? Give it to me, if you please.'

He honoured her outspoken thought and handed it to her in silence.

'I received it two days ago,' he said.

'One word only,' answered the Poetess, as she unfolded the letter—a short note written in a small, cramped hand. 'Have you any tidings of your model?'

'None,' he replied. 'Only that I believe that letter to be from her, and I did not wish to show it to any but yourself.'

She began to read the lines slowly and carefully, and Sybil knelt by her side.

There was a long pause. Then the Poetess rose and returned the letter; the power of a great determination shone in her earnest eyes.

'That letter has relieved me of an additional burden,' she said with a wan smile, 'Now my course has become more clear before me. I must go to Italy soon.'

'Why?'

The exclamation came naturally from both her hearers at once. She resumed her seat and answered quietly,—

'Mr Vernon, that letter is, as you say, from her —Lucia—I mean—why should I shrink from saying it? from my mother. She writes it to tell you that she regrets the disturbance which she created in your house, after your kindness to her. She speaks of the deed she has done as a climax for which she has lived and worked—which for years she has been anticipating. The whole idea of her life seems to have been that of revenge— the only revenge possible to her.'

The rich voice trembled a little over the words —she paused a moment to steady it.

'There is nothing more in the letter, Mr Vernon, except a mere statement that the writer is now on her way back to her native land, and to Florence. She writes defiantly, boldly. There is nothing that can at all palliate her crime, nothing that can draw from you any sympathy. And yet, Mr Vernon, although the thought of her must, as far as you are concerned, be always fraught with pain and annoyance, yet I would ask you to blend some mercy, if you can, with your just severity. You do not know all the circumstances; it is perhaps right now that you should.'

'Yes,' he answered very gently, 'if it is your pleasure.'

His heart was torn with pity and reverence for the girl who bore her part so bravely, and with a bitter feeling of shame that his dead friend whom he had honoured should in any way have proved unworthy of his trust. And as he listened to the story which fell from Michal's lips—the same story that had been already told so differently by the separate actors in the drama—the sense of justice and an unconquerable pity strove within him still.

'Ichabod is written over the memory that till now has been so pleasant,' he said at length in a low voice, full of feeling. 'This is all very sad to me; I could not have believed it.'

'Would that I were not obliged to force the belief upon you,' Michal answered gravely. 'The knowledge of my parents has been thrust upon me in an unexpected and most singular way. I might have known my father's name years ago had I cared to do so, but I chose ignorance, and now the revelation has proved more painful than I dreamed.'

'Since when have you learnt all this?' asked Leslie Vernon quietly.

'The day before yesterday. His—Lord Trevelyan's—lawyer wrote to me, and I went to see him at once. From him I heard that just lately, within the last few weeks, Lord Trevelyan had made some alterations in his will that affected myself'—she paused; the subject was painful to her sensitive pride, but the artist, in his keen interest, urged her to continue. 'He has settled the estate of Illingford upon me,' she went on hurriedly, 'and an income that suffices. I could ask no more. I have nothing to complain of; but there is one duty left for me to fulfil.'

'And that?'

'To find my mother,' she said simply; and the artist noted, with a vague feeling of wonder, that while she spoke of her father as of a stranger, the tenderer relationship, with all its drawbacks, seemed to arouse in her less pain.

He said nothing; the thought was very startling to him; he could not bring himself to associate his wild Italian model with the girl he so reverenced and admired.

'Yes, it seems to me,' she continued slowly, 'that the claim of a mother is an eternal claim. It can never be annulled or cast aside. It appeals to us as no other relationship can do. My quest may be useless, it can but be painful, and yet I feel bound to undertake it. Do you understand? Perhaps, with Aurora Leigh, I too have "felt a mother want about the world so long."'

'Yes,' he answered thoughtfully. 'I think I understand. It is what I should have expected from you.'

'Mr Vernon!'

He looked up, and saw that she was crimsoning under the influence of some agitating thought.

'Mr Vernon—I forgot. I spoke inconsiderately. This matter lies more properly in your hands. The letter has given you a clue on the track of a criminal—the murderer of your friend. Without it, the police may fail to find her. At present it appears that they have found no clue. Do you consider it your duty to give them this information?'

He started, and his lips framed a hasty negative, but she went on hurriedly, as though a task had been set her to perform.

'She has sinned against the laws of civilised humanity,' she said, and her low, sweet voice trembled upon the words. 'She has sinned against the higher laws, which we call God's. I must put it plainly, though it is very terrible to me.'

'Oh! Poetess!' Sybil, who was still kneeling by her friend's side, raised her head in sudden distress and terror. 'Oh! Poetess! Mr Vernon; you could not! it would be too dreadful, and what good in the end?'

'Hush!' said Michal, a little sternly; 'that is for Mr Vernon to decide. Each one must judge for himself of his duty.'

But her hands were trembling as she spoke.

Leslie Vernon was greatly moved when he answered her in a grave tone.

'Miss Murray says truly I could not do it, and I think that there are sufficient reasons.   The woman who has done this deed is not mad, neither is she likely to extend her malice, or do any one else any harm.   That malice was concentrated, as it seems, upon one person.   She has suffered the greatest wrong that a woman can suffer at the hands of a dishonourable man, and in her passionate nature love turned to hate and an overwhelming desire for revenge.   In such natures it is ever so, and no execution of justice, no prosecution of law against her, can remedy what has been done.   Neither does the fear of the law trouble her; her letter proves her to be reckless of herself and of her safety. Her sin is upon her own head.   Her condemnation under our laws would satisfy what we call our justice, but it would not be likely to soften that fierce, passionate nature that knows so little of the higher, nobler life.   No, I will give no clue to the authorities who are seeking for her; they must find her without my help, or not at all.'

'I knew you would say that,' murmured Sybil, and the Poetess looked at him with a grave, sad smile.

'Your thoughts are mine,' she answered gently, 'and I thank you for your brave expression of them. I do not think it very likely that they will succeed in tracking her to Florence. No one seems to have known her whereabouts in London, with whom or where she lived. By this time she has probably arrived in Florence. For myself, as I said, I must follow in the faint yet earnest hope that some external influence and sympathy may, after all, bring into her life some light, some happiness that she has hitherto never known. That is my aim and my hope.'

'You will start for Italy shortly?' he asked with as much unconcern as he could muster.

Michal looked up at him with thoughtful eyes.

'Yes, I think so. There is nothing to prevent it; and do you not think that the change will be of infinite benefit to Sybil?'

'Undoubtedly,' he answered, and his assent was eagerly seconded by Sybil herself, to whom the idea of the journey, despite its painful errand, was alleviated in a slight degree by this suggestion of benefit to her art.

Michal read the conflicting thoughts in her bright eyes, and smiled lovingly.

'To me also it will, in one sense, be a great joy,' she said softly. 'I feel again with Aurora — "I would have seen thee sooner, Italy, for I have heard thee crying through my life."'

'Perhaps you will never return,' said Leslie Vernon.

'Oh, yes, we shall!' cried Sybil. 'We must return. I am sure the thought of perpetual exile, even in that enchanted land, would not please either of us; would it, Poetess? Say we will return.'

'Darling child! of course we shall hope to return,' said Michal brightly. 'You forget, I must not neglect my English home.'

Her face became suddenly clouded, and the artist, watching her, divined the cause.

'I believe you would rather have been free from that estate,' he said suddenly.

'Yes,' she answered without hesitation, 'I am so unused to anything of the kind; I dread the care and responsibility,'

'You might sell or let it,' said he.

She shook her head.

'That seems cowardly. I would rather have the satisfaction of knowing that the place was well kept and beautifully ordered; that the land was thoroughly cultivated, and the people thoroughly cared for. That is a landowner's duty; but at present it all seems very difficult to me. I shall go and see the place before we leave England, and perhaps we shall soon learn to love it very much.'

'I think you will.'

The artist brightened. Some few hundred yards of English soil did not appear such an insurmountable barrier to friendly intercourse.

'There is one person for whom I feel intensely,' said Michal, after a pause. 'And that is Lady Trevelyan.'

The artist laughed.

'Indeed! That is, I fear, compassion misplaced.'

'I think not,' she answered quickly. 'I know nothing of her personally, but, from what I have seen and heard, I feel sure that all this—this *dénouement*—"scandal," I suppose the world will call it—must be a very severe trial to her. And she is innocent of it all. She also has suffered wrong, and now her proud name is in everyone's mouth, handled freely, I doubt not, in those deadly instruments of venom and vulgarity—the "Society" papers. It is humiliating to think of it, and she must feel it bitterly, for I am told that she is ill.'

'I am sorry; I may have judged her harshly,' said Leslie Vernon, and he began to talk lightly of other things.

But, as he pursued his way homewards, his thoughts dwelt again upon that approaching separation with a dull sense of pain. He tried to rejoice with the girls in the anticipation of a new and sweet experience, but for him the world had suddenly grown grey. One voice only echoed within his consciousness. '*Eutbehren sollst du— Sollst eutbehren*,'* it cried to him ; it was the voice of his own lament.

* Thou shalt be deprived.

CHAPTER XXV.

'’Tis but a worthless world to win or lose ;
So hath it proved to thee, and all such lot who choose.’

CHILDE HAROLD.

POOR thing,’ said London Society. ‘How very dreadful for her! Poor thing!’

And with many protestations of affection and sympathy, London Society called daily at Lady Trevelyan’s door.

But beyond the usual civil reply to such sympathetic inquiries, it could hear nothing, and went away with curiosity unabated and a sense of vexation unappeased.

Rumour was, as Michal had correctly surmised, very much afoot. After travelling round the usual curriculum of falsehood, and picking up variations and amendments at every turn, it finally began to grow weary of a scandal so vague and undefined. For the fire that sent up such volumes of smoke into the social atmosphere was indeed but a feeble glow, and London Society, unable to penetrate

253

the mystery, lost heart, and satisfied its pharisaic
conscience by throwing exaggerated blame and
pity upon all the people concerned. It levelled
some subtle abuse at Leslie Vernon, whom everybody knew so little and was therefore so free to
criticise; it spoke in carefully-worded phrases of
the widowed Countess; it moralised upon the crafti-
ness of the murderer and the Nemesis of revenge.
But as rumour grew into an established fact, and
the identity of Michal become assured, London
Society was unable to resist the temptation then
offered, and indulged in many ill-natured comments that were calculated to wound the pride
and the feelings of Norah Trevelyan. Not that
that mattered in the least, for the Countess was
commonly believed to have no feelings. But in
this Society erred, for she was feeling it all intensely, this proud and lonely woman who, sat
day after day alone in her rooms feverishly con-
ning over the paragraphs wherein her own fair
name appeared. She insisted that all the papers
should be brought to her; she read and re-read
them constantly, and the words, however meaning-
less, seemed to pierce her soul. She would see
none; to her servants she was, as usual, distant
and composed; her illness was no physical ailment to be cured by the physician's art, it was
the sickness of 'a mind diseased.' But one day

she received a letter. It was, she thought, a very
remarkable letter, and she read it many times with
a mixed feeling of repulsion and surprise. It bore
the simple signature of *Michal;* it was written in
a style at once so dignified and gentle, so self-
contained and yet so genuine in feeling, that it
appealed to her world-worn consciousness as something fresh and new. In spite of herself, her
prejudice gave way a little ; she began to ask herself whether it would not, after all, be better to
feign at least an outward show of intimacy with
this girl, whom, in her altered position, Society
would not be slow to recognise. After some consideration she adopted this view of the case, and
wrote a peremptory note of invitation. She was
not prepared to be cordial, but in her loneliness
and dejection the interview seemed more possible
to her than it would have done before.

Nevertheless, the entrance of Michal upset her
preparations, and took her by surprise. As the
girl came slowly towards her, erect and calm, she
began to realise that this was not a person to be
either conciliated or put down. With instinctive
courtesy she rose and held out her hand, murmuring a few words of greeting.

And the girl, looking straight into the beautiful,
weary eyes, could find nothing but pity in her
heart for Norah Trevelyan ; pity that the Countess

would bitterly have resented had she guessed its existence, but which might have betrayed itself in the sweet sympathy of Michal's voice, and the softness of her eyes.

'We are not entirely strangers,' she said, as she seated herself in a low chair and caressed one of the tiny spaniels who came sniffing at her gown. 'We met one evening at Sir John Charlecote's—at dinner.'

'I believe we did, though I hardly recognise you. I do not remember faces very easily. It is kind of you to come to-day. I should not have thought of asking you but for your letter. Then I thought it might be as well.'

The broken utterance was strange in her, but she felt restless and ill at ease.

'I think it is only right that we should meet,' said Michal gently. 'From the beginning—since the 4th, I mean—I have felt intensely for you in your trouble, though for me, too, the days have brought much perplexity, much grief.'

Norah Trevelyan watched the earnest face furtively. There was no possibility of misunderstanding here, she thought There was a grand directness of aim and purpose in Michal which she felt instinctively to be genuine.

'You never knew who your father was until a few days ago?' she said abruptly

'I did not.'

'Well, it was no loss to you, and now it is gain. You will live at Illingford, I suppose, or is it your intention to live in London?'

'You ask me a hard thing,' said Michal, smiling. 'It is not easy to map out one's future life at so short a notice. I have only one plan immediately in prospect—that is my journey to Italy.'

'Indeed!'

Michal, looking down, did not catch the cold smile of irony in her companion's eyes.

'I hope that the land of romance may prove less fatal to you than to your father.' Then, with a sudden change of tone, she added, 'I wish to know something of your life hitherto. I cannot quite understand with whom you have lived.'

So Michal told her simply the story of her life; spoke tenderly of the fatherly care and love which had surrounded her; of the generous environment in which her energies had found full play, and in which her ambition had silently developed.

And Norah Trevelyan, with curious eyes still scanning her companion's face, listened with scanty interest to the brief narration.

It was all very commonplace, she thought, like everything else in the world. Perhaps the girl herself was commonplace also, in spite of the aristo-

R

cratic head and the deep, fathomless eyes. She gave a half-impatient sigh.

'Well, I daresay you will find Illingford a suitable *pied à terre* when you are married,' she said indifferently. 'The shooting is excellent, and the society around everything that you could desire.'

'Yes; but what if I do not desire it?' said Michal gently. 'Would you consider the estate thrown away upon so insensible a person?'

'I do not understand you. Do you belong to a sisterhood, or are you going to convert the house into a nunnery?'

'I hope not.' Michal hesitated under the inquisitorial glance of the cold, blue eyes. 'But neither will I convert it into a rendezvous of fashionable society,' she continued with some warmth. 'If I find friends they shall be welcome, but I will not spend my time and money in entertaining crowds with whom I have no sympathy at all.'

'I expected, when I became aware of your parentage, to find you somewhat unique,' said Norah Treveylan coldly; 'but I daresay these opinions are only the result of your monotonous life; you will become like other people in time. It really is a mistake to affect singularity.'

An unusual depression swept over the Poetess and held her mute. She was beginning to realise the immensity of the gulf that may separate human beings from each other; the entire absence of sympathy that no amount of effort, of speech, of persuasion, may ever, in the faintest degree, overcome. Such dissimilar minds may live side by side for ever as strangers, for ever misunderstanding and for ever misunderstood.

And Michal, feeling this acutely, was silent from very despair. In her strong, all-embracing sympathy, she had longed to do something or say something that might touch the heart of the woman whose exterior was so polished and cold; but she began to feel that it was impossible. The next remark of the Countess took her by surprise.

'I wondered whether you were perhaps the author of this book,' she said, taking a small volume from the table by her side. '*Poems by Michal Iliff*— that was the name by which you were known, I believe?'

'Yes,' answered the girl simply.

'I thought so; the book was brought to me with others from the library. I have not read it—I do not care much for poetry; besides, I have not been well lately. I want a change.'

'I am sure you do.' Michal rose and looked down sadly at the pale, beautiful face. 'Perhaps, she said hesitatingly, 'when I return you will let me see you again?'

'I shall not be here,' said Norah Trevelyan. 'I do not intend to stay in London in any other position but that which I formerly held. I am going back to Wales to my own place and my own people. Lord Treveylan's brother takes the title, as I daresay you know. For my own part, I have done with a family who appear to be only capable of disgracing themselves and everybody who belongs to them. You, of course, are not to blame. If that Italian savage is ever found, I suppose we may anticipate further complications. However, so long as I am far removed from the scene of action, I care little how the course of events may run.'

Her face belied her words; the haughty disdain and passionate scorn with which she had first listened to the Earl's confession had gathered again upon her brow. Michal saw it and understood.

'I know,' she said in a low tone, her own face crimsoning with humiliation and pain,—'I know how terrible it is, and must be, to you; but, forgive me, you will outlive it; it is the innocent alone who can outlive the consequences of error, and I think it is they who deserve all the consideration that the world can bestow upon them. Who knows? You may find truer love, truer sympathy awaiting you now than any you have found hitherto.'

Norah Trevelyan took the hand extended to her

in silence, and looked . doubtfully into the great dark eyes.

'I am glad I have seen you,' she said, quietly. 'Good-bye, Lady Michal.'

And the Poetess, seeing her gesture of dismissal, had no choice but to go.

CHAPTER XXVI.

'Lo! thou hast won a treasure, angel pure;
See that thou art worthy.'

GLORIOUS in the amber light of morning, its palaces and towers shimmering in the sunshine like opals in a crystal sea, its woods and gardens clothed with the tender emerald of new-born foliage, lay the city of the Medici—Florence the Fair.

On that steep hill, whose summit is crowned by the old Etruscan buildings of Fiesole, a solitary stranger stood looking down upon the enchanted scene. Life was all astir around him. Bright-eyed peasants passed him by unheeding as they sauntered to their pleasure or their work. The breath of the morning, fragrant with the suggestion of orange and myrtle, leapt over his brow as though in welcome. He greeted it in speechless joy.

Around him were the gardens of those bright villas which are so thickly sown upon the sloping hills; at his feet, the beautiful buildings of the city raised their vivid landmarks against the still, blue sky.

The stranger's glance travelled perpetually over those shining outlines, resting now upon the triumph of Brunelleschi, the vast cathedral dome; now upon the rich belfry of Ghiotto, the steeples of Santa Croce and St Mark; tracing also, beneath the bridges, the course of the silent Arno as it stole on through peaceful pastures to the sea.

He lingered over the scene in a transport of wonder and delight.

'Florence!' he cried, 'Florence!'

It affected him strangely. In the magic of that moment he was living a new life; the past, with its sorrow was no more. With a mist before his eyes he turned and began to descend towards the city, and, on looking at his watch, wondered to see that it was nearly nine. He had walked for two hours, and had had no breakfast, but he did not remember that now.

As he neared the Porto Gallo, he showered some coins upon the beggars who asked for alms. Joy is ever liberal,—in his mood of exaltation, he could sympathise with all the world.

Soon he passed the gate; he was now in Florence; he laughed aloud in his gladness, like a child. It was many years since he had traversed the once-familiar ground; many changes had occurred since then, and in some uncertainty, he took a circuitous route to the Piazza del Gran Duco. In this time-honoured spot, where so much of the interest and beauty of fair Florence is concentrated, the stranger paused and looked around him.

Opposite, stood the Pallazzo Vecchio, with the great fountain of Neptune by its side; on the left the bronze equestrian figure of Cosmo de Medici towered upon its pedestal, and, on the right, the graceful proportions of the Loggia stood out against the sky. He looked round at it all in silent delight for some minutes; then he started again across the broad Piazza in the direction of the Loggia di Lanzi.

How glorious the world seemed to him on that summer morning under that sunny sky! His vivid fancy, borrowing the roseate hues of his joyousness, invested each statue, each stone, with a golden aureole of thought. The streets were of crystal, the houses of mosaic; he himself was the ransomed prince set free from captivity to dwell in the land that he loved.

The sea-god, rising, giant-like, among his spirited ocean steeds, seemed to look down upon him with a welcome; the David of Michael Angelo gave him gentle greeting, and he gazed with a newly-awakened admiration at the Hercules in his colossal strength. Then he ascended the steps into the Loggia, looking straight before him with softened, dreamy eyes.

He stood in the circle of coloured marbles, surrounded by those gems of sculpture which Florentine genius has bestowed upon the world; there he was free to luxuriate in those old-world representations, and in the memories which they awoke. He drew a long breath as he glanced around him. There was the bronze Perseus of Benvenuto Cellini, and the corresponding group in marble on the other side.

Near the latter a few people were standing, tourist-wise, with guide-books in their hands. One was a tall woman. He noticed, with dreamy appreciation, the graceful sweep of her black dress as she stood with her back towards him.

Then suddenly she turned.

The tourists who were standing by at that moment forgot the marble Sabines in the more vivid momentary interest excited by the little human drama just being enacted under their eyes. Who or what were these people, they wondered, as they saw the man spring forward with shining, eager eyes, and noticed the stately movement of the girl in black, who went forward to give him greeting. Lovers, perhaps, said the tourists; lovers who had been separated for many years, and who had at last met among the statues in the Loggia. It was really quite romantic.   They returned to their guide-books, satisfied.

'Poetess,' cried the stranger, as he sprang forward; and then, as he caught her hands and held them tightly, he seemed to have no more to say.

The girl, bending her grave, inquiring glance upon him, saw that he was altered; the gladness that suffused his countenance, the joy that lighted up his eyes, was a new birth hitherto unknown. The girl's heart beat quickly. With a sudden, intuitive knowledge she divined the meaning.

'You are come,' she said slowly, with a little catch in her voice that betrayed her emotion, 'to tell us—yes—I know it—you are free!'

In the silence that followed his brief assent, the girl moved slowly away from him.   The balance of her mind was trembling; she felt the impossibility of speech.   And yet, why should it have been so difficult at that supreme moment to rejoice unconditionally at the thought of her darling's happiness. It would surely be happiness—it must be.   This man, who had fulfilled the sweet duties of friendship so honourably, would not fail in honour now. He was worthy; she could not doubt it.   And now he had come to her with that wonderful gladness shining in his eyes—his whole soul filled with the radiance of hope, of joy, of anticipation—

and how could she withhold her sympathy from him?

No; she would give it loyally, gladly. It was only the suddeness of the news that had overcome her; only the faint stirring of regret that forces from some earnest souls, as from St Paul, the exclamation,—'I would that all men were even as myself.'

She shook off the feeling with a revulsion of passionate shame. It was unworthy, it was selfish; her love must rise superior to such egotistic dreams.

She went again to the spot where the artist still stood. She was very pale.

'Mr Vernon,' she said softly, 'I rejoice with you. I sympathise,—I am glad—glad—*glad.*'

The emphasised reiteration of the word gave her a strange satisfaction. It was as though she spoke to convince herself, not him, of her sincerity.

'Thank you,' he answered. 'I knew that you would say that. I have been dreaming of this moment ever since I knew—'

'When did you know?' she asked gently.

'Last Friday. I started on Monday for Florence. I could not rest till I had told you—till I heard what you—and she—would say.'

They had descended the steps of the Loggia and were walking, as if by mutual consent, in a westward direction towards the Ponte Vecchio.

'Did you hear any particulars?' continued the Poetess.

'Not many. They simply wrote to tell me that my wife had died. They said that at the last she was peaceful.'

'That, at least, is something for which to be thankful,' answered Michal in a low tone.

He nodded, and there was a pause.

'And when did you arrive here?' she asked smiling. 'I am a true mark of interrogation this morning, but you must excuse it, as you have come upon me unawares.'

He laughed. There was a ring of mirthfulness in the laugh that made it pleasant to hear.

'I came last night,' he said, and I went to the Hotel de l'Arno—close by here, you know. I started quite early this morning to Fiesole. I walked there and back—I had been walking all the time before I met you.'

'All the morning? But it is now ten o'clock. Where did you take breakfast?'

He laughed again, with a careless 'abandon' of indifference.

'I declare we have changed places oddly,' he cried. 'I can never again laugh at you for your absent habits. I forgot that there was such a thing as breakfast in the world.'

'You will return with me at once,' she answered,

'and have some. Such irregularities cannot be allowed, even in Florence.'

He hesitated. The eyes that looked inquiringly into her own were so full of meaning that Michal answered the unspoken thought.

'Sybil is painting in one of the galleries,' she said with a little smile. 'You can go to her if you like, or see her later.'

'Later, then,' he replied, with a world of joy and of gratitude in his eyes.

He asked no questions about Sybil; there was nothing at that moment that he cared to say. As Michal led on towards their lodging, talking as she did so about many indifferent things, he followed in supreme content. It was wonderful to be walking by her side in this city of Art and Poetry, to be listening to the music of her exquisite voice, and to know that, presently, the little, happy face that he had seen and loved in his dreams would greet him with a smile.

Deep joy is oftentimes but a clumsy orator; it sits in awkward silence while its sister Sorrow, like Philomela under the poplar tree, flings her lamentations far and wide. It is uncouth in manner, and does not recommend itself to the stolid gaze of practical men. The world in general eyes it askance, with a whispered hint of Bedlam. But the Poetess, who had drunk deep at the fountain of

humanity, had a place in her heart for joy.
She excused all the artist's monosyllables, mis-
fitting though they often were, and she talked
on for the sake of sociability, desiring no intelligent replies.

But when they had reached the little sitting-
room where, for the last four weeks, she and Sybil
had found so pleasant a home, and she began to prepare a light repast for her visitor, the artist's con-
versational powers revived. It was now his turn
to question, and, with some hesitation in his voice,
betokening a keen and earnest sympathy, he bade
her tell him the result of her painful quest. Simply
and without reservation she told her tale. It was
indeed a relief to her to speak of it to the only
person in the world besides Sybil who knew all
the circumstances and would understand.

'My quest is ended,' she said gravely, 'and I
have a memory to carry away with me during the
remainder of my life that will amply compensate
for all the sacrifice and all the pain.'

'You have found her, then?' he said eagerly as
she paused for a moment and he saw that her
emotion was very strong.

'I found her,' she answered. 'Just as I had
hoped to do, in this beautiful Florence, in the
same little house where she had lived so many
years. I found her ill—very ill—stricken with

fever and raving in delirium, and I stayed with her—to the end?'

'The end!' he repeated in grave inquiry.

She bowed her head in assent.

'My knowledge of my parents has, in both cases, abruptly ended, she said with a sad little smile. 'I knew from the first that there was no hope of my mother's recovery; it was for me only to try if perchance my presence might soothe the few last hours of her restless pilgrimage. I never left her, though for the first week it seemed as though my quest had been indeed in vain. She knew no one— she asked for no one. In her incoherent ravings she seemed to be at war with all the world. Oh! I can hardly speak of that week to anyone! I was glad to have even Sybil away from me—you do not know how dreadful it all was.'

The artist looked at her with intense sympathy. She was hardly aware of his presence; it seemed to her that she was again standing in that little room, by the bedside of the mother whom she had never learnt to know, listening helplessly to her wild, incoherent ramblings.

So helpless she had felt! with a heart so full of yearning for just one glimpse of the mother love that should surpass in strength all other human attributes—so full of tender pity for the poor, erring soul that could triumph only in the empty gratification of its long sought and terrible revenge.

'And the end? was there nothing to repay you?' asked Leslie Vernon very gently.

'Repay me,' she answered, with one of her rare, rich smiles. 'Yes, it repaid me, Mr Vernon—it was worth while. There came a day—it was the last but one—when I, still watching, saw a flash of reason leap into her eyes and knew that the time had come for me to tell her that I was Michal, her child. At first she did not seem to understand it, and, having understood, she did not seem to care. That was the most terrible thing to me—that she, though deprived as she had been of her natural rights and privileges, should, at the last, have no feeling left for me. But gradually—oh! how good it was to recognise—the absent sense seemed to awake in her, and the memory of those few last hours is very precious to me. I can at least remember that my presence was a comfort to her— that she liked me to be near. Some softening influence—I cannot tell what—seemed to have settled upon her; perhaps the memory of her girl-hood had returned, and obliterated for the time the sense of revenge and wrong; perhaps even the knowledge which I tried to teach her—of my motive in finding her out, may have accounted for it in some degree. Anyhow, it was so. The anger and bitterness of years had left her, and I believe that she regretted that last fierce act of revenge.'

'You were right; it was worth while,' said the artist gravely. 'You have cast oil upon the troubled waters, and now, "after Life's fitful fever, she sleeps well." To how many troubled human lives is not that a fitting epitaph?'

Michal did not answer, and the subject was dropped between them for that day.

In after years, the girl did not often recur to it; the remembrance of that dying mother was a thing too sacred to be often spoken of; and of all that had passed between them, no one, not even Sybil, knew. There are things that lie beyond the reach of the truest friendship, and the strong soul stands alone in the supreme moments of its life.

After a long silence, the artist rose and went up to the window where Michal was standing looking down into the narrow, busy streets beneath.

'You are very happy here,' he said, looking smilingly into the grave, dark eyes.

'Yes; it has been very peaceful, very sweet; but it must not last much longer. There are duties that call me to England again.'

'You regret that,' he said quickly. 'I see it in your eyes,'

'I cannot deny it,' she said smiling. 'Do you remember that little simile of Browning's—

"I used to sit and look at my life as it rippled and ran
  Till, straight before,
  A great stone stopped it!"

That is my case: the "great stone" is my new position. It has come suddenly upon the peaceful ripple of my life, and I can no longer pursue the even course straight onward, but am forced to turn aside. By-and-by all will be easy, I have no doubt. The path to all truest success lies through renunciation, and the future may yet grant to me more days of beauty in my beloved land.'

'The future holds many a crown for you, Poetess,' he said gravely. 'Do you know what *England* is saying of your book?'

She coloured slightly, and looked at him with grave and thoughtful eyes.

'I know,' she said simply, 'and the praise of my readers is a cup of mingled pleasure and pain. See—a book is but a dewdrop in the vast firmament of human effort; it is born of the eternal elements which are for ever being aggregated into complex forms, and separated again into simple. It is kissed into existence by the sun of imagination which colours all human thought; it is evanescent as the rainbow, and yet, in some form or other, it will continue till the end of Time. This dewdrop of mine is one of the least among its brethren. It will be my great endeavour to produce another work that shall be worthier of men's praise.'

'How do you think to attain to that higher excellence?' asked Leslie Vernon thoughtfully. 'By study, I suppose, and the mental discipline accruing from steady work.'

'Partly,' she answered. 'I think that the study of an author should be the strong foundation on which the superstructure of his imaginative thought must be balanced. A life that is to benefit its fellow-men must train itself to habits of patient application. It must "listen long" before it may attempt to sing. Such study is like the "foot" of the embryo fern, which it plunges into the prothallium to derive therefrom its sustenance, till, gradually, it can uncoil its own sweet leaves, fair and stately, when the appointed time has come.'

'Yes, it is all law,' said the artist. 'Universal, inexorable law.'

'I think it is all God,' said the Poetess slowly. 'The Power of the First Cause—of the Founder of this vast system, which at all points we may touch but cannot govern, filters through all the universe. It meets us at every turn of our lives. The religions of the world have all had this one aim—to bring us into contact with that mysterious power, that unseen God. Worship is inherent in humanity, inquiry is inevitable, and the symbols of man's worship have changed and will change with the different ages of the world. Only the one thing which the ignorant Hindoos sought, and we—still ignorant—seek to-day, will surely stand for ever, and at the last our longing eyes will open upon the Eternal Light of Truth.'

'I believe that too,' he answered gravely, and a short silence followed.

The exuberance of his former mood had passed away from him, giving place to a hesitating diffidence. He glanced again at the face of the Poetess; it was very noble, very calm. She met his glance and smiled, and the smile was full of sympathy. He took her hand gently in his own.

'Lady Michal,' he said, with a feeling that the formal address somehow placed a gulf between them, 'do you remember what you said to me one evening many months ago, when I came to you and told you my story? Do you remember saying, in speaking of your treasure, that the prince of her affection, if ever he should come into her fair young life, must be worthy of her?'

'I remember it,' she answered.

His eyes sought hers in wistful pleading.

'And now—that I have come again to you, to tell you that I am free—that I would give my life to serve her—that I love her as did Dante, Beatrice—as Petrarch, Laura—that I would be content to wait, if only—'

A movement on her part checked his halting utterance; the gulf that his imagination had built up fell asunder before the direct glance of her earnest eyes.

'I told you that I was glad for you when I heard your news,' she said gravely. 'And I tell you now, truly, that if you win her, as I think you will, I shall be glad for her also.'

'And—for yourself,' he ventured timidly.

She smiled.

'Have I not said enough?'

'Yes; forgive me. You have said everything that you could say—enough to make me proud and happy all my life, and humble too, knowing how little I deserve it. Only I know that marriage is not your ideal life; I think you do not look upon it, as do most people, as the *summum bonum* of a woman's existence, and I thought—'

He hesitated, and smilingly she filled the broken gap.

'You interpret me so far correctly,' she answered. 'It is indeed the crown of many lives, but it can never be of all. The fact which the world is so slow to recognise is that of the diversity of gifts, of mind and of character, which make the same scheme of life utterly inappropriate to all. There are women to whom the system of marriage, with its unqualified surrender, its gigantic sacrifice, and its responsibilities must be for ever impossible—the age has not yet arrived when the pressure of such surrender shall be removed. But in the meantime, there are women also who wear their responsibilities so loyally, and who fulfil their sacred duties with such loving care that the fragrance of their lives endures for generations. Such are the women who alone should be the mothers of our children. To me, as you know, this life would be impossible, but with my little girl it is otherwise. I have no fear for her, or—for you.'

And the artist, listening with bowed head, silently made an inward vow at that moment that her trust in him and in his loyalty should never be betrayed.

CHAPTER XXVII.

*'Life's fadeless crown is twisted from the leaves
Of little flowers of love.'*—WADE ROBINSON.

THE valley of the Arno lay sleeping in the full, white sheen of the moon; tender filaments of silver played on the great cathedral dome, and glanced across from spire to palace in a glistening web of light.

All vivid colour, all the bustle of the noontide life had faded into the calm of that universal radiance and repose. Earth had sunk into insignificance, and the dusky canopy of heaven glowed with the infinite splendour of the planets and the lesser stars.

From the terrace gardens, behind the Pitti Palace, the course of the river could be discerned, flowing like a streak of crystal amid the surrounding mists of blue.

This was the spot which the artist had chosen, and hither, in the evening, he led the girl who held his fate so lightly in her gentle hands. He had found the two girls at home and awaiting him upon his second visit, and Michal had proposed that he and Sybil should take a walk together, she excusing herself on the ground of slight fatigue.

With a little reluctance and some wonder, Sybil yielded, and so it came to pass that Leslie Vernon found himself wandering by the side of the girl whom he loved, in the beautiful gardens of Boboli. And there, among the statues that embellish those secluded walks, there where the scent of the myrtle lingers among the bowers, and every nook is peopled with the memories of a gorgeous past, the artist, in the clumsy utterance of intense feeling, told the old-world tale. He was not eloquent; he was only very much in earnest, and somewhat timid withal, for he had lived hitherto in an atmosphere of such stern self-repression, he had accepted the calm conditions of their friendship so absolutely, expecting nothing more, that the sudden realisation of his banished dream was as strange as it was sweet.

And Sybil felt it equally.

She stood before him with drooping head and eyes filled with wonder, while he was eagerly yet timidly watching for a glimpse of those downcast eyes, to read therein his answer.

Presently she looked up, and the eyes were soft

and shy, and a tiny, rippling smile made the sweet lips curve in lines of wondrous beauty.

That one little smile worked a miracle in the life of Leslie Vernon. It gave him a glimpse of a future than which no dreamland was more fair—a future whose moments of satisfied content would obliterate the memory of sorrow-laden years.

Oh! those years! Never again would he remember them, never again regret their anguish, for he had surely emerged from the Valley of the Shadow of Death into the glorious Palace of Joy. He looked down at the sweet face with its happy eyes uplifted to his own, and he passed his hand over his brow like a man who has been accustomed to darkness and for whom the light of heaven is too strong. The soft touch of her curls thrilled him as her head rested upon his shoulder. She was his own, his Beatrice; and he, like Dante, stood gazing into her pure, transfigured eyes in the radiant light of Paradise.

Yes, it was his Paradise—these green garden ways, where the bright-eyed lizards peeped and sparkled under the calm, resplendent sky—this was a place where the soul might rest and be satisfied. He lifted his uncovered head in the moonlight, and raised his eyes to the dusky Heaven. There, Arcturus and Orion, Sirius and the Pleiades, looked down upon him, the little stars twinkled in the blue.

'My little girl,' he said gravely, and the throbbing tenderness of his voice brought a mist before her eyes. 'My little flower, so fresh from God, I dedicate the remainder of my life to you. You have been my joy, my love, my compensation. Henceforth I have no will, no thought, but yours.'

'Hush,' she answered gently, in the shy and tender voice he loved so well, 'we will have no sacrifice. The most perfect unions are those—are they not?—where the individuality is not sacrificed, though the love is unchanging and true?'

'My Beatrice,' he murmured softly. The self-distrust, born of his scarred and blighted past, awoke in him the passionate and chivalrous desire to serve, however humbly, the lady of his love. 'I can offer such a poor return for your beautiful young life,' he said sorrowfully. 'My own has been so full of blunders—so seared by the contrary winds of Fortune—it is not worthy of you, my little girl.'

Her light laugh stole upon his ear like music.

'If *I* think it is, that should be enough for you,' she answered brightly. 'Why, you silly man, it is just the fact of those past "blunders" being over and gone that makes the present happiness so perfect. If you had been happy and prosperous all your life, I don't think I should have cared for you one bit.'

He listened, and the sweet truth fell like balm upon his soul.

As they walked together slowly through the pathways where the tall, thick hedges of evergreen rose on either side, the silence was broken again by a small, caressing voice,—

'I could not leave the Poetess, could I?' it said softly, and the artist was startled from his reverie.

'Leave the Poetess! why, my darling, you might as well think of leaving your art. No, my feeling is rather one of intense joy and gratitude to think that our lives may always have the privilege of close contact with a character so beautiful as hers.'

'That is right; I knew you would say so,' said Sybil with shining eyes. 'And it does not matter where we live. Oh, I think it is lovely to live anywhere!'

Her light-hearted tenderness roused him gradually into a less contemplative mood, and as they wandered slowly together through the fair Italian city by night, their talk grew more eloquent, imaginative and free.

They were treading on the same ground that the poets and artists of old had trodden with the heroes and the Saints of Florentine history. Those statues, those palaces—the genius of Fra Angelico,

of Andrea del Sarto, above all, of Michael Angelo,
speaks from those decorated walls! Yonder is the
St Mark of Donatello, that the great master
commanded to 'Speak.' Here is the house of
Machiavelli, and yonder surely we may see the
grave, level brows and gleaming eyes of the Divine
Poet as he lingers near his beloved Baptistry with
its glorious gates of bronze.

Here, too, in bitter contrast to the Medicean
glories, rises the memory of that terrible outrage,
in which the martyred monk Savonarola expiated
his love for the tumultuous and passionate Floren-
tines. In the high tower of the old Palazzo, he
looked out day after day upon the streets and
houses of the beloved city, flanked by the purple
hills and snow-clad Appenines. In that same
piazza, finally, the last scene of the tragedy was
enacted which stands out as an event so significant in the history of all time.

The thoughts that lie in the heart of Florence
are long and winding thoughts. Out of the
stones the great dead speaks to us—we recognise
them, and call them all by name. Each house has
an interest for us. We say,—'This and that man
was born here,' and 'this and that deed was done.'

But the old Florence, with its throbbing, restless
life, has passed away for ever, and we build each
epoch of our advancing civilisation upon the

crumbling, yet eternal fabric of the past. 'Every epoch, says Mazzini, 'is organic. The progressive evolution of the thought of God, of which our world is the visible manifestation, is unceasingly continuous. The chain cannot be broken or interrupted. The various aims are united together—the cradle is linked to the tomb.'

CHAPTER XXVIII.

'This is the right method of proceeding towards the doctrine of Love—beginning from these beautiful objects here below, ever to be going up higher—mounting from the love of one fair person to the love of two, and from the love of two to the love of all, and from the love of beautiful persons to the love of beautiful employments, and from the love of beautiful employments to the love of beautiful kinds of knowledge, till he passes from degrees of knowledge to that knowledge which is the knowledge of nothing else save the absolute Beauty itself.'

(THE 'SYMPOSIUM' OF PLATO.—(*Jowett's Translation.*)

MANY years passed peacefully after that evening spent by Sybil and Leslie Vernon in the Boboli Gardens of Florence—years which brought to them the blessings that every individual covets—peace, prosperity, and honour among men.

The moving calendar left small trace upon the active and cheery presence of Leslie Vernon. The comrades, who rarely in former years exchanged a syllable with him, said now with a jest and a smile that *his* marriage at least must surely have been made in Paradise, seeing its exhilarating effect upon him.

The jest, on reaching his ears, provoked a laugh, mirthful and tender withal, for there was a nucleus of truth in it which he was ready to confess to all men.

He was not then, and never had been, an idealist; he knew that a life-companionship was the only true test of love, and that, in all marriage, as in all friendship, the barriers of the real press closely upon the individual life, and the ideal, with its dreams of perfection, lies outside in the region of the unattainable.

But he was too true a philosopher to murmur at the inevitable limitations of humanity, and, moreover, too thoroughly satisfied with his own happiness to be covetous of more.

The fair little life that daily unfolded to him its graces of rectitude and purity was, even as he had said, his compensation and his joy, and under its influence, his art had expanded into new paths of originality and vigour. The age which, in his first flush of genius, had crowned him with its praise, now offered the incense of enthusiasm at the shrine of his work. And it was the truest test of his power that he did not yield to its temptations, and become its favourite or its slave. He laboured, not for the public, but for the dignity of his profession; The vial of his cynicism was always ready to be poured out upon the former, but Art alone was the mistress whom he humbly tried to serve. With Sybil it was not so.

Handicapped by her regard for public opinion, she was not able to soar above the region of mediocrity. Art, like Literature, is a jealous mistress, and will have a whole heart or none. And little Sybil, in her joy-giving and joy-desiring nature, had not found it possible to limit her energies thus; she would work often in happy content by her husband's side, rejoicing in his genius, and basking in his tender praise, but the restless ambition of her girlhood had lost itself in the wider ocean of her love. They lived in the beautiful old Hall of Illingford; the tenants of Lady Michal. Here they spent the greater part of the year, with occasional visits to their beloved Florence. The labourers and farmers who lived on the estate of Illingford had a genuine respect for the grave and kindly master, who took so deep an interest in their welfare and their work. They welcomed also the sunny presence of Sybil, whose merry laugh so often echoed through the corridors and in the cosy, pannelled Hall. But it was with a simple reverence —that feeling so akin to worship, which we yield instinctively to something higher and nobler than ourselves—that the people of Illingford saluted Michal. Years only added to her stately beauty, giving her earnest brow a look of deeper seriousness, of calmer thought. Of her the world has ever spoken, and will ever speak, with reverence; and fashionable Society, following blindly the lead of its judges, laid traps for her in vain. Lady Charlecote, possessed with an unabated admiration for 'poor Frank's ward,' never rested for an instant from her matrimonial schemes. She was strongly inclined to take to herself the entire credit of Sybil's marriage.

'If I had not asked the girls to my house, how on earth would they have got on?' she said, vaguely, but with some asperity, to her husband; and Sir John knew better than to dissent.

So the lively little lady, in company with Norah Trevelyan, who had reappeared in Society as the wife of Lord Elcoe, made schemes for the marriage of Michal, and will probably go on making them to the end. With the delicious freedom of people who criticise a subject without understanding any of it, they reviewed the '*intérieur*' of the Illingford household, and liked it little. But the Poetess herself, in that infinite patience and gentleness with which a larger mind submits to be misunderstood, because it cannot bear the probing touch of an alien, had a gentle word and smile for all. She lived her own life truly and earnestly as the guardian of her glorious gift; those who valued her work knew something of that life's rare beauty,

T

but those who lived in close contact with her knew and loved her best.

For every great poet and great genius should be immeasurably greater than his work; he must be calm and liberal in thought, generous in sympathy; such an one makes quiet and continual progress over the rough stepping stones of human effort that lie in the broad river of Life.

It was thus and ever thus with Michal. Smaller souls, coming ever and anon to draw from the inexhaustible well of her friendship, found in the pure draught wisdom and content; and thoughtless lives, lighted by the Promethean torch of her inspiration, would be roused instinctively to follow in her tread.

Such are the stately pioneers of our progress; they pass, and drift beyond our ken, but their influence is an eternal link in the ascending chain of Humanity. 'Only the Time shadows,' says the Idealist of Chelsea, 'have perished, or are perishable; the real Being, of whatever was and whatever is and whatever will be, *is* now and for ever.'

Surely: let us 'take' heed therefore, how we sow.

THE END.

London: DIGBY, LONG & Co., Publishers,
18 Bouverie Street, Fleet Street, E.C.

DIGBY, LONG & CO.'S NEW NOVELS, STORIES, Etc.

IN THREE VOLUMES, Price **31s. 6d.**

By DORA RUSSELL.

A Hidden Chain. By the Author of "Footprints in the Snow," "The Other Bond," etc., etc. In Three Volumes, crown 8vo, cloth, 31*s.* 6*d.* [*Second Edition.*

By JEAN MIDDLEMASS.

The Mystery of Clement Dunraven. By the Author of "A Girl in a Thousand," etc. In Three Volumes, crown 8vo, cloth, 31*s.* 6*d.* [*Second Edition*

By PERCY ROSS.

The Eccentrics, By the Author of "A Comedy without Laughter," "A Misguidit Lassie," "A Professor of Alchemy," etc. In Three Volumes, crown 8vo, cloth, 31*s.* 6*d.* [*Just out.*

By GILBERT M. F. LYON.

Absent Yet Present. By the Author of "For Good or Evil." In Three Volumes, crown 8vo, cloth, 31*s.* 6*d.* [*Just out.*

By MADELINE CRICHTON.

Like a Sister. In Three Volumes, crown 8vo, cloth, 31s. 6d. (SECOND EDITION.)

The *GLASGOW HERALD* says:—" The writer possesses the faculty of depicting character with force and consistency. The literary texture is good, and the dialogue throughout is brisk and vivacious."

IN ONE VOLUME, Price **6s.**

DORA RUSSELL'S LATEST NOVEL.
(THREE VOLUMES IN ONE.)

The Other Bond. By the Author of "A Hidden Chain," "A Country Sweetheart," etc., etc. Crown 8vo, cloth, 6*s.* [*Immediately.*

NEW NOVEL BY TIVOLI.

Une Culotte: or, the New Woman. By the Author of "A Defender of the Faith." With Six Original Illustrations, by A. W. COOPER. Crown 8vo, cloth, 6*s.* [*Just out.*

18 *Bouverie Street, Fleet Street, London.*

NEW NOVELS AND STORIES—*Continued.*

NEW NOVEL BY EDITH GRAY WHEELWRIGHT.

The Vengeance of Medea. Crown 8vo, cloth, 6s.
[*Just out.*

NEW NOVEL BY EMILY ST CLAIRE.

A Ruined Life. Crown 8vo, cloth, 6s. [*Just out.*

NEW NOVEL BY IVON HAMILTON CAMPION.

A Dawnless Fate. Crown 8vo, cloth, 6s. [*Just out.*

NEW NOVEL BY ALGERNON RIDGEWAY.

The Westovers. By the Author of "Westover's
Ward," "Diana Fontaine," etc. Crown 8vo, cloth, 6s.
The *GLASGOW HERALD* says:—"The "Westovers" is a clever book.

NEW NOVEL BY COLIN CLOUT.

Norman, or, Inherited Fate. Crown 8vo, cloth, 6s.
The *SHEFFIELD DAILY TELEGRAPH* says:—"A well-considered plot,
and several characters firmly drawn."

NEW STIRRING TALE OF ADVENTURE.

The Flaming Sword. Being an Account of the
Extraordinary Adventures and Discoveries of Dr
PERCIVAL in the Wilds of Africa. Written by Him-
self. Crown 8vo, cloth, 6s.
THE SPEAKER says:—"Mr Rider Haggard himself has not imagined more
wonderful things than those which befell Dr Percival and his friends."

NEW EXCITING TALE OF ADVENTURE.

Lillieville. A Tale of Adventure. By MAURICE J.
SEXTON. Crown 8vo, cloth, 6s. [*Just out.*

NEW NOVEL BY JOSEPH BRADBURY.

First Devenport of Bramhall. By the Author of
"A Lost Name," "The Ardennes of Arden Hall,"
"Grace Barton," etc. Crown 8vo, cloth, 6s. [*Just out.*

Deferred Pay: or, A Major's Dilemma. By
Lieut.-Colonel W. H. M'CAUSLAND. Crown 8vo, cloth,
6s. (SECOND EDITION).
The *SCOTTISH LEADER* says:—"A more than usually interesting novel.
There is plenty of incident and adventure, and not a little fun. The story gives a
soldier's life from a soldier's point of view."

Her Angel Friend. By MONICA TREGARTHEN. Crown
8vo, cloth, 6s.
The *MANCHESTER EXAMINER* says:—"Most admirably conceived and
executed."

NEW NOVELS AND STORIES—*Continued.*

England against The World: A Novel. By JOHN LITTLEJOHNS, Author of "The Flowing Tide," etc. Crown 8vo, cloth, 6s.

The *SCOTSMAN* says:—"His readable and enjoyable novel. .... Threads of adventure, romance, and love, which one may pursue with considerable interest."

In Due Season. By AGNES GOLDWIN. Crown 8vo, cloth, 6s.

The *ACADEMY* says:—"Her novel is well written, it flows easily, its situations are natural, its men and women are real."

IN ONE VOLUME, Price **3s. 6d.**
By HUME NISBET.

Her Loving Slave. By the Author of "The Jolly Roger," "Bail Up," etc., etc. In Handsome Pictorial Binding, with Illustrations by the Author. Crown 8vo, cloth, 3s. 6d. [*Just out.*]

Pipe-Lights. Being a Collection of Random Thoughts concerning a variety of Subjects. By HAROLD T. WHITAKER. Crown 8vo, cloth, 3s. 6d. [*Just out.*]

A Son of Noah. By MARY ANDERSON. Crown 8vo, cloth, 3s. 6d. (FIFTH EDITION.)

The *GUARDIAN* says:—"To have told the love story of Shem in Biblical phraseology is a deed worthy of the highest admiration, and we cannot sufficiently congratulate the authoress on the undertaking, for she has really succeeded in making it interesting. There is an excellent description of a fight with a mashtak, and the account of the Deluge is very vivid."

The Hero of the Pelican; An Ocean Drama. By PERCY DE LISLE. Crown 8vo, pictorial cloth, 3s. 6d.

The *PEOPLE* says:—"There is some really good writing in this volume, and the author seems to have the makings of a second Clark Russell."

The Girl Musician. By MIRIAM YOUNG. With full-page illustrations by MATTHEW STRETCH. Crown 8vo, cloth, 3s. 6d.

The *LIVERPOOL MERCURY* says:—"This is a very pleasing story. The book is quite delightful."

The Old House of Rayner. By GRIMLEY HILL. Crown 8vo, cloth, 3s. 6d.

The *DAILY TELEGRAPH* says:—"Eminently readable. .... Written to entertain ... Fulfil their object very adequately."

The Last Cruise of the Teal. By LEIGH RAY. In handsome pictorial binding. Illustrated throughout. Crown 8vo, cloth, 3s. 6d. (SECOND EDITION.)

The *SPECTATOR* says:—"The stirring tale of sea adventure which the book contains is told well and graphically enough to be very readable."
The *NATIONAL OBSERVER* says:—"It is long since we have lighted on so good a story of adventure."

NEW NOVELS AND STORIES—*Continued.*
IN ONE VOLUME, Price 3s. 6d.

The Bridal March. From the Norwegian of Björnson, and **The Watch**; an Old Man's Story. From the Russian of Ivan Turgenieff. Translated by JOHN EVAN WILLIAMS. Crown 8vo, cloth, 3s. 6d.

The *LITERARY WORLD* says:—"'The Bridal March,' with its vivid descriptions, will be read with interest. . . . Charmingly told, the characters are skilfully drawn, and stand out in strong relie. . 'The Watch' is replete with vigorous touches, and wholly original. It exhibits the writer's peculiar gift of character drawing, supplemented by effective descriptive power."

Keith Kavanagh Remittance Man. An Australian Novel. By E. BALDWIN HODGE. Crown 8vo, cloth, 3s. 6d.

STAR.—"The story is excellent, the dulness of an Australian bush station in winter being an admirable piece of description

The Bow and the Sword. A Romance. By E. C. ADAMS, M.A. With 16 full-page drawings by MATTHEW STRETCH. Crown 8vo, pictorial cloth, 3s. 6d.

The *MORNING POST* says:—"The author reconstructs cleverly the life of one of the most cultivated nations of antiquity, and describes both wars and pageants with picturesque vigour. The illustrations are well executed."

IN ONE VOLUME, Price 2s. 6d.

Lost! £100 Reward. By MIRIAM YOUNG, Author of "The Girl Musician." Crown 8vo, cloth, 2s. 6d.
[Just out.

Clenched Antagonisms. By LEWIS IRAM. Crown 8vo, cloth, 2s. 6d.

The *SATURDAY REVIEW* says:—"'Clenched Antagonisms' is a powerful and ghastly narrative of the triumph of force over virtue. The book gives a striking illustration of the barbarous incongruities that still exist in the midst of an advanced civilisation."

My Village. By R. MENZIES FERGUSSON, M.A., Author of "Our Trip North," etc., etc. Crown 8vo, pictorial cloth, 2s. 6d.

The *LITERARY WORLD* says:—"This is an interesting book. The scenes depicted will revive in many breasts enchanting memories of bygone years, and obscure villages far away."

Dr Weedon's Waif. By KATE SOMERS. Illustrated with full-page drawings by MATTHEW STRETCH. Crown 8vo, cloth, 2s. 6d.

VANITY FAIR says:—"One of the prettiest and most touching stories we have read for a long time."

NEW NOVELS AND STORIES—*Continued.*

For Marjory's Sake: A Story of South Australian Country Life. By Mrs JOHN WATERHOUSE. In handsome cloth binding, with illustrations. Crown 8vo, cloth, 2s. 6d.

The *LITERARY WORLD* says:—"A delightful little volume, fresh and dainty, and with the pure, free air of Australian country parts blowing through it . . . gracefully told . . . the writing is graceful and easy."

IN ONE VOLUME, PAPER COVER, Price **1s.**

A Stock Exchange Romance. By BRACEBRIDGE HEMYNG, Author of "The Stockbroker's Wife," "Called to the Bar," etc., etc. Edited by GEORGE GREGORY. Crown 8vo, picture cover, 1s. (TENTH THOUSAND.)

Our Discordant Life. By HENRI D'HÉRISTAL. Crown 8vo, picture cover, 1s.

A Rash Vow. By TAMAN SHUD. Crown 8vo, picture cover, price 1s.

A Police Sergeant's Secret. By KILSYTH STELLIER, Author of "Taken by Force." Crown 8vo, picture cover, 1s. (FIFTH THOUSAND.) [*Immediately.*

DIGBY'S POPULAR NOVEL SERIES.

In Handsome Cloth Binding, Gold Lettered, Crown 8vo, Price **2s. 6d.** *each, or in Picture Boards, Price* **2s.** *each.*

BY JEAN MIDDLEMASS.

The Mystery of Clement Dunraven. By the Author of "A Girl in a Thousand," etc. (SECOND EDITION.)

BY DORA RUSSEL.

A Hidden Chain. By the Author of "Footprints in the Snow," etc. (SECOND EDITION.)

BY DR ARABELLA KENEALY.

Dr Janet of Harley Street. By the Author of "Molly and her Man-o'-War," etc. (SEVENTH EDITION.) With Portrait.

BY HUME NISBET.

The Jolly Roger. By the Author of "Bail Up," etc. With Illustrations by the Author. (SIXTH EDITION.)

NOTE.—Other Works in the same Series in due course.

MISCELLANEOUS.

The Autobiography of an Old Passport, 1839-1889, chiefly relating how we accomplished many Driving Tours with our own English Horses over the Roads of Western Europe before the time of Railways. By the Rev. ALFRED CHARLES SMITH, M.A., Author of "Attractions of the Nile," "A Spring Tour in Portugal," "A Pilgrimage through Palestine," etc. With numerous illustrations. Royal 8vo, cloth extra, 21s.

The *DAILY NEWS* says:—" There is a refreshing flavour in these chatty Diaries . . . these lively and amusing reminiscences. . . . There is nothing in the tours and trips of to-day to compare with them in charm."

Leading Women of the Restoration. By GRACE JOHNSTONE. With portraits. Demy 8vo, cloth, 6s.

The *LITERARY WORLD* says :—"This is a very readable book. . . . This book, indeed, contains a few valuable lives, told fully and fairly, of women who deserve to be remembered."

Three Empresses. Josephine, Marie-Louise, Eugénie. By CAROLINE GEAREY, Author of "In Other Lands," etc. With portraits. Cr. 8vo, cloth, 6s. (SECOND EDIT.)

The *PALL MALL GAZETTE* says:—"This charming book. . . . Gracefully and graphically written, the story of each Empress is clearly and fully told. . . . This delightful book."

Winter and Summer Excursions in Canada. By C. L. JOHNSTONE, Author of "Historical Families of Dumfrieshire," etc. With Illustrations. Crown 8vo, cloth, 6s.

The *DAILY NEWS* says—"Not for a long while have we read a book of its class which deserves so much confidence. Intending settlers would do well to study Mr Johnstone's book."

The Author's Manual. By PERCY RUSSELL. With Prefatory Remarks by Mr GLADSTONE. Crown 8vo, cloth, 3s. 6d. net. (SEVENTH AND CHEAPER EDITION.) With portrait.

The *WESTMINSTER REVIEW* says:—". . . Mr Russell's book is a very complete manual and guide for journalist and author. It is not a merely practical work—it is literary and appreciative of literature in its best sense; . . . we have little else but praise for the volume."

18 *Bouverie Street, Fleet Street, London.*

MISCELLANEOUS—*Continued.*

A Guide to British and American Novels.
From the Earliest Period to the end of 1893. By PERCY RUSSELL, Author of "The Author's Manual," etc. Crown 8vo, cloth. Price 3s. 6d. net.

GLOBE says—"Is unquestionably useful"
MORNING POST says—"Will be of considerable value."
MANCHESTER COURIER says—"An invaluable storehouse of facts."
NEWCASTLE CHRONICLE says—"·The Guide may be recommended to librarians as well as to readers of fiction."

Sixty Years' Experience as an Irish Landlord.
Memoirs of JOHN HAMILTON, D.L. of St Ernan's, Donegal. Edited, with Introduction, by the Rev. H. C. WHITE, late Chaplain, Paris. Crown 8vo, cloth, 6s. With Portrait.

The *TIMES* says:—"Much valuable light on the real history of Ireland, and of the Irish agrarian question in the present century, is thrown by a very interesting volume entitled 'Sixty Years' Experience as an Irish Landlord. . . .' This very instructive volume."

Nigh on Sixty Years at Sea. By ROBERT WOOL-
WARD ("Old Woolward"). Crown 8vo, cloth, 6s. With Portrait. (SECOND EDITION.)

The *TIMES* says:—"Very entertaining reading. Captain Woolward writes sensibly and straightforwardly, and tells his story with the frankness of an old salt. He has a keen sense of humour, and his stories are endless and very entertaining.

Whose Fault? The Story of a Trial at *Nisi Prius.*
By ELLIS J. DAVIS, Barrister-at-Law. In handsome pictorial binding. Crown 8vo, cloth, 3s. 6d.

The *TIMES* says:—"An ingenious attempt to convey to the lay mind an accurate and complete idea of the origin and progress and all the essential circumstances of an ordinary action at law. The idea is certainly a good one, and is executed in very entertaining fashion . . . Mr Davis's instructive little book."

Charlotte Corday; or, a Hundred Years After.
By MARY JEAFFRESON, Author of "Roman Cameos," "Through all the Varying Year," etc. Crown 8vo, cloth, 2s. 6d.

The *DAILY CHRONICLE* says:—"Young and beautiful, of good birth and breeding, accomplished, lonely and sad, with a silvery musical voice, and a lovely vision of some ideal republic of all the virtues and all the talents—Charlotte Corday is one of the most attractive figures in history."

18 Bouverie Street, Fleet Street, London.

POETRY.

Fragments of Coloured Glass: Poems and Ballads, Historical, Religious, Australian and Miscel laneous. By ALPHONSUS W. WEBSTER. Crown 8vo, cloth 5s net. [*Just out.*

The Feast of Cotytto, and other Poems. By CHARLES T. LUSTED, Author of "Studies in Life and Literature." Fcap. 8vo, cloth, 3s. 6d.

The *DAILY NEWS* says '—"The poem from which the collection takes its name is a little masterpiece. The verse moves to perfect music, and to such a variety of it as makes it seem to dance on its course."

Sir Dunstan's Daughter, and other Poems. By ALFRED SMYTHE. Author of "The Warlock," etc. Crown 8vo, cloth, 3s. 6d. With Portrait.

VANITY FAIR says:—"A pretty tale well told in poetry. Throughout the verse is exceptionally good."

Poetry, the Press and the Pulpit. By A Village Peasant. Crown 8vo, cloth, 3s. 6d.

The *COURT CIRCULAR* says:—His thoughts are well expressed, and there is the ring of true poetry."

Some Translations from Charles Baudelaire, Poet and Symbolist. By H. C. With Portrait. Fcap. 8vo, elegant parchment, 2s. 6d.

The *TIMES* says:—" Are executed with no little metrical skill and command of poetic diction."

*** *A complete Catalogue of Novels, Travels, Biographies, Poems, etc., with a critical or descriptive notice of each, free by post on application.*

www.ingramcontent.com/pod-product-compliance
Ingram Content Group UK Ltd.
Pitfield, Milton Keynes, MK11 3LW, UK
UKHW051602270125
4307UKWH00052B/1962